Candor

Candor

How to have courageous coaching conversations
when it really matters

Steven J. Stowell, Ph.D.
Tony I. Herrera, Ed.D.

CMOE Press
Salt Lake City, Utah

CMOE, Inc.
9146 South 700 East
Sandy, UT 84070

ISBN-13: 978-0-9724627-8-5

First Edition
Printed in the USA
Text Editing: Helen Hodgson, Emily Hodgson-Soule, Cyndi Keller, and Josh Nuttall
Cover Design: DTS
Typesetting: Josh Nuttall

This book and other CMOE Press publications are available on Amazon.com, BarnesandNoble.com, and by ordering directly from the publisher.

CMOE Press
+1 801 569 3444
www.CMOE.com

ACKNOWLEDGEMENTS

We want to thank everyone who assisted us in this unique writing journey. We recognize that turning the *Courageous Coaching Conversations Workshop* into a book was a team endeavor and want to thank all who made it possible.

- Each member of the CMOE design team for pulling the pieces together and for their dedicated efforts in making this book a reality.

- Craig Weber for his early introduction to these ideas and concepts and his many years of thought, leadership, and guidance.

- Our partners at Schreiber Foods, for their courage and willingness to put these ideas into practice daily.

- Helen Hodgson, our long-time editor. We appreciate her diligence, talent, and input.

- Our families who, as always, were so patient and supportive during this creative process.

Table of Contents

INTRODUCTION

As companies strive to engage and motivate the workforce, inspire collaboration, and coach people to contribute more to the business, you—as leaders—are challenged with different roles and are looking for new models. To be effective in your roles, you face an assortment of daunting responsibilities that you must successfully execute. These challenging tasks include providing rigorous performance feedback to people who may not want it, making tough decisions under pressure, consistently holding people accountable for their performance, and acting as a clear, vibrant channel of communication between senior management and the rest of the workforce.

When it comes to effectively performing these vital functions, one pivotal skill stands out above all the rest:

having the ability to foster potent, direct, constructive dialogue—even when the issues are difficult, uncomfortable, and complex. You cannot afford to simply focus on managing tasks and technical issues while relying on human resource departments to deal with people. Leaders must focus on fully developing their team members, as well as regularly providing them with guidance and feedback.

Like most leaders, you are smart, committed, and hardworking. Your intentions are almost always good. You want to address issues and concerns, but you also want to eliminate tension and stay comfortable, even when you are preparing to deliver a decidedly uncomfortable message. Unfortunately, you can't often have both. The tradeoff is that the more comfortable you are during these tense conversations, the less effective you become in delivering the message you intend to convey. You know what needs to be said, so why is it that when you are confronted with challenging situations, your tendency may be to withdraw? Instead of fulfilling the demands of these difficult circumstances, you may choose to ignore the problem and avoid giving direct feedback, guidance, and coaching to others. What is going on?

Chances are that you do want to raise an issue or speak your mind, but you don't want to polarize the conversation, make yourself or others uncomfortable, be seen as a troublemaker, or be labeled a "non-team player." You genuinely want to work with others to solve problems, but you want the problems to be defined and solved your way. More often than not, when an important conversation does not go the way you had hoped, you tend to blame the other party for your lack of progress. Likewise, when the interaction goes well, you tend to take personal credit for its success, attributing the positive outcome to your own personal prowess. This is called "self-serving bias." It takes strong presence of mind to step back, look at the situation, and ask, "What am I doing to contribute to the shortcomings of this conversation?" You must take personal responsibility for your ineffectiveness, which can make even the toughest leader a little squeamish.

These serious, necessary conversations are made more difficult by a variety of variables. When important issues are finally addressed—perhaps after months or years of being ignored—both parties are likely to experience a great deal of discomfort. You may also have some tacit (subconscious) intentions lurking behind the scenes. In this case, you're unaware of your true motivations. But while they may have faded into the background, they significantly impact how you approach important discussions. When you engage in essential, but challenging discussions, you often truly are of two minds: One part of you wants to have a direct, open discussion about the issue at hand; the other part is concerned about getting into trouble, looking like a jerk, and either experiencing discomfort yourself or causing pain to others. You want to be clear and direct, but you also want to be non-confrontational, keeping the tension low and any bad feelings or negative emotions to a minimum. Why do these sorts of conversations tend to be so difficult? Why do you have so much trouble being effective, even when you give your best effort? Why do most leaders find these conversations so threatening?

The purpose of this book is to answer these questions. We will help you explore the importance of using candor to have effective, powerful conversations about your most important issues and challenges—particularly when solving business problems, helping team members learn, and providing coaching and feedback to others. We have used a fictionalized case study to make our points. It adopts a "you" perspective to allow you to take the role of Adrian, a senior manager at Galaxy Corporation. Adrian explores a situation that develops as a result of ineffective coaching conversations with a departmental manager and what needs to be done after the fact. Although this is a work of fiction, the circumstances surrounding the issues explored in this book are likely to be familiar to most people in positions of leadership.

Candor: How to have Courageous Conversations when it Really Matters strives to help leaders appreciate the vital importance of having effective conversations about challenging subjects, recognize the defensive tendencies that often hamper such conversations, and explore and practice a tested framework for facilitating balanced conversations under stress (i.e., when tensions are high or the topic is controversial).

As leaders of people ourselves, we have spent decades working in the trenches, struggling to help teams within a variety of organizations. We have been students of leadership, and we have conversed with and coached thousands of leaders in over 50 countries. We wrote this book because we believe that the concepts and powerful framework we share in the following pages will help you develop vitally important leadership skills. Courageous conversations using candor are the keys to strategy, innovation, execution, and sustainability. Courageous conversations are a critical lever for employee engagement, commitment, and satisfaction. Courageous conversations are good for people, good for teams and organizational dynamics, and good for business. Our personal experiences working in positions of leadership inspired us to become avid proponents of this message.

The book you hold in your hands was influenced by the brilliant work of Chris Argyris and Donald Schoen, whose research on Action Science has spanned nearly 50 years and may be considered some of the most robust social-science research ever conducted. Our contribution to their efforts is intended to provide a more thorough understanding of, and user-friendly approach to, their model, its complexity, and its numerous applications. Candor is not about changing others as much as it is about identifying and correcting ineffective patterns of communication when guiding, coaching, and giving feedback to others. This courageous conversations concept is not a gimmicky set of oversimplified steps to follow. Instead, it is a robust skill set that requires awareness, focus, discipline, and consistency in order to be effective. Just like learning to play a musical instrument, mastering a foreign language, or perfecting skills in a new sport, gaining the ability to engage in skillful, courageous coaching conversations takes a high level of commitment, resolution, and a lot of practice.

The 5-step courageous-conversations process found in Chapter 7 is not a panacea; we won't claim that candor is a silver bullet for solving all of your conversational challenges, and it certainly won't fix all of your business woes. What it does do is provide a framework to help guide you through the dialogue. We will help you identify and overcome the predictable conversational patterns that have developed over time. Regardless of your age, sex,

race, socioeconomic background, or title in the organi-
zation, you can fall into traps that can cause you to have
disappointing, unproductive conversations with others.
Candor is a guide to developing a new set of skills that
will increase your conversational competence, bring your
natural tendencies to light, and give you something to
hang on to when emotions run high. We hope you enjoy
the journey!

ONE

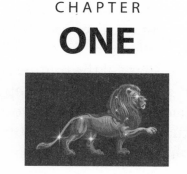

Galaxy and Lee

Your morning is starting out a little strangely. Normally, you are an early riser. The quiet of the early morning allows you to take a few minutes for yourself, get your day organized, and check your e-mail. On mornings when you aren't too buried with projects, you even take the time to do a light workout. But this morning is different. You can feel it when you open your eyes. As you lie in bed, your restless mind starts working. You know you have to get moving, so you roll out of bed and walk over to look in the bathroom mirror. You stare deeply into your own eyes and think, "Adrian, this is going to be a tough one." You contemplate the big day ahead of you, and the challenging conversation that will occur later in the day during your monthly leadership meeting with your boss and peers is at the forefront of your mind.

Sometimes these meetings are difficult, but they are always candid and honest. Everyone speaks their minds; no one is afraid to challenge and hold each other accountable for doing their share of the routine activities, as well as the long-term strategic tasks. You appreciate receiving honest feedback, and you give it to your colleagues in turn. You actually like the competitive spirit in the team because Galaxy loves results; it needs results. It is a younger, smaller company than many of its competitors in the industry, and it has to leverage every opportunity it can. However, you and your colleagues thrive in this environment. Success for an underdog simply means you have to run a little harder and be a little smarter in the way you use your resources, engage your people, and shape the future. You are used to these challenging discussions. This isn't the first time you and your business-development team have been put under the microscope by your business-unit leader and peers.

But something feels different about today, and as you are working out on the treadmill, it clicks. Last week, two of your peers from Operations and another person from Customer Service asked you the same question: "How is Lee, your marketing manager, really doing? Is she coming along, or is she struggling in her new role?" Alarmingly, each person had made that query on a different day. You sense that a key part of the conversation at the leadership-team meeting today will be about Lee.

As you board the train for your regular commute to work, you attempt to formulate your thoughts regarding where you stand with Lee. You know the leadership team well, and you know that this afternoon's discussion is going to be intense. They will ask you about everything that's taking place in Marketing and whether or not Lee is up to the task of reshaping the department. You know that you'll need to be prepared for the onslaught of questions to come. You are fully aware that the results the senior leadership team is looking for from Lee just aren't there yet, and everyone is getting worried.

As you sit on the train, your mind drifts back to a year ago and the conversations about the vacant marketing job that had taken place between you and your boss. Everyone had agreed that Scotty, Lee's predecessor, had to go. Scotty had been unable to effectively launch and market a new product. He had failed to engage his team and build morale, constantly went over budget, and was a master at making excuses and blaming others. When you finally sat down with Scotty, it hadn't been a difficult conversation. He knew why you were calling him into your office just after the beginning of the New Year. And as it turned out, everyone on the team was pretty excited that you had had the courage to roll Scotty off the team. Once he was gone, you learned that most people in the organization had found Scotty difficult to work with.

Nearly everyone in the organization wanted to move Galaxy forward at a faster pace. Some big, new, exciting product offerings were being rolled out. They had the potential to become blockbusters in the industry and put Galaxy on the map. Everyone felt that this was Galaxy's big moment. The excitement in the air was palpable. People were finally beginning to realize that Galaxy had a shot at achieving its vision; this was their chance to play in the big leagues, if only they could research, produce, market, and sell their products more effectively than their competitors could. Everyone's hopes hinged on successfully introducing Galaxy's hot new product, Zarium, in the coming months. Zarium is a powerful new compound that the R&D group had been working on for years. It had passed its final trials, and the drug was ready to be manufactured and taken to market. But when it came time to market the drug, it became clear to everybody that Marketing was the weak link and the decision to make a change was the key to success.

The lights flicker as your train passes through another tunnel. You think about the call you had made to Michael, your favorite headhunter, when Scotty's position opened up. Michael was excited. The market was flush with talent, and he knew that he could find at least a dozen outstanding candidates for the open position at Galaxy. These were talented professionals who would fit into Galaxy's culture and long-term strategy. They were more than capable of beginning to contribute right away. You remember how excited you were as you began sorting through some of the résumés early in the year. As you discussed the marketing role with your human resource manager, you quickly settled on three candidates and invited each of them in for face-to-face interviews. They all looked good on paper: great qualifications, top-notch educations, and solid work experience. Later, as they made the rounds through the senior-leadership team, it seemed clear that one candidate stood out from the others: Lee.

Virtually everyone agreed that Lee was the most qualified applicant. You, in particular, had loved her energy. She seemed like a hard-charger and a go-getter, someone who would take Marketing by storm, but also be able to strike a balance between working long hours and being committed to her home life. Her qualifications fit the position perfectly; she had an MBA from a great school, and she'd punched all the right tickets after graduation. You were especially impressed with the fact that she had made the sacrifice to go overseas early in her career to gain some international exposure. She went to a tough geographic area—the Middle East—where business was booming. It would not have been easy for a young, professional woman in that part of the world, but she had shown a dogged determination and the persistence needed to make her experience in the Middle East a success. When she came back to North America, she took a sales position in Canada and learned to speak passable French. She worked directly with customers. She solved problems on the front lines. In Canada, she quickly turned a sales team around that had perpetually been in last place.

During her interviews, you quickly saw that she builds relationships with others masterfully, has an outgoing personality, and is very responsive to problems. This was exactly what Galaxy needed in marketing: somebody who knew the challenges of working with difficult customers, the importance of good sales tools, and key ways to motivate a team for success. Frankly, you were so excited about Lee that you could hardly contain yourself.

When you held your second interview with Lee, you were candid with her. You told Lee that Galaxy had some big challenges ahead of it. You made it clear that the previous team leader had had some problems and that Lee would need to rebuild the team's morale. You told her that she would have to overcome numerous departmental issues, such as a corporate audit that wasn't closed yet. You shared that the budget for Marketing was a mess and that the training program and first round of sales literature

for Zarium had been disastrous. Lee would have a pile of immediate problems that needed to be fixed, and you needed her to know it.

Ultimately, what Galaxy needed most from a marketing manager was a forward-looking vision and a sense of the possibilities for Galaxy in the long run, and you hoped Lee would be able to fill that role. You thought it seemed obvious to Lee that Galaxy was at a turning point, changing from a small player in a niche market into a company that had a shot at becoming the next major player in the pharmaceutical industry. This would be a heavy burden for any new manager. There was a lot to fix in the short term, but at the same time, you needed a marketing manager who could start positioning Galaxy more strategically. You needed a manager who could move beyond the next drama situation waiting to unfold in the marketing team.

When the Marketing department had started to unravel, the leadership team had vigorously debated its future. Some members of the team simply wanted the near-term marketing headaches to go away. They would have been happy to just have Lee put out the fires. Others wanted a more progressive, forward-looking, long-term strategic leader—not just a firefighter. Lee had probably heard from both sides during her interviews, and you felt confident that she had gotten the message: You needed results both today and in the future. At least, you thought that Lee had understood that you needed a doer as well as a shaper. Galaxy's unique situation required a marketing manager who could not only manage the day-to-day marketing functions, but also think strategically, exercise discipline, and avoid getting sucked into the activity trap.

You needed someone smart enough to invest time, talent, and resources in preparing Galaxy for the next big opportunity, someone who could build a marketing team that would be ready for anything down the road. At any rate, as the Senior Director of Sales & Marketing at Galaxy Corporation, you find that thinking about all of the challenges you're facing with Lee now is giving you a headache.

TWO

Adrian Sees the Problem

t the office, you settle into your usual routine and forget about the whole Lee situation for a little while. Several vendor appointments and conference calls fill most of your morning. Fortunately, one of your district sales managers missed his flight and won't be in for his monthly review, and one of your conference calls has been postponed until next week. So you have a little time to catch up on a few strategic issues of your own. You take the opportunity to slip away from all of the office chaos and spend a little time thinking in one of the break rooms. You have a lot to think about. You need to figure out how you would accommodate the impending growth in the company if Zarium becomes a blockbuster pharmaceutical. You would need to increase your staff tremendously, and you aren't sure where you would put all the new talent. You also need to decide if the current information-technology system would be sufficient if the company were to double in size. In the break room you make a hot cup of herbal tea as thoughts continue to run through your mind. You need to take stock of your own strategy. If Zarium does take off, what would the sales force look like in the future? What kinds of new technology would you need? Which new competencies would the Galaxy workforce need to acquire? You settle into a comfortable chair in the break room, and as you think through these issues, your mind drifts back to Lee. You know you will be asked some serious questions during the leadership meeting this afternoon, and you have to be prepared.

It is not unusual for these meetings to go deep and consume the entire afternoon—"death by meeting," as some have called it. This group wants the nitty-gritty details, and as a leadership team, you have agreed to operate this way. Members of this team don't just manage their function. Everyone has a whole-enterprise point of view. If one person is having a problem, that problem belongs to everyone. During these meetings, every member of the team brainstorms solutions, comes up with new ideas, and provides input and advice. But once the ideas have been offered, it is up to the individual to implement the idea, execute the plan, and produce measurable results.

You settle down with your notebook and stare out the window; your mind wanders back to your dilemma with Lee. Admittedly, you like Lee. You picked her for this position for a reason. You believe that she's smart and capable, but you also know that you have pinned a lot of hope on her. And after the disappointment with Scotty last year, your expectations for Lee are very high.

You are the first to admit that Lee deserves a lot of credit. She relocated her family for this job and gave up a good position at another company for an opportunity to make a difference at Galaxy. In some ways, you actually felt a little sorry for Lee when she was hired; you knew that for the first few months, this job would be a tough slog. But you had hope. You were confident that she could get on top of all the pressing issues pretty fast. You realized when you hired her that Lee was fairly young for this leadership position, and this would be her first big opportunity to guide an entire team. Lee had honed her leadership skills working in the trenches and on the front lines. But that is what you wanted. You needed somebody who understood how things worked in a business from the ground level up.

You sip your tea and think about the last nine months, concluding that during her first three months, Lee had hit the ball out of the park. "Look," you say to yourself, "she didn't waste any time. She took on the financial audit, crunched all the numbers, and made tough decisions." During her review of the files, Lee had also discovered that one of the team members working closely with Scotty had violated company policies and ethics. She then concluded that he, like Scotty, had to be let go. That was good. You respected Lee a lot for having the courage to make a tough decision to address an issue that had been hindering the day-to-day performance of the entire team.

Then, Lee sat down with the Learning and Development people and ironed out a number of training problems that the sales team was having due to confusing product messaging. The following month, Lee found a good off-site facilitator, and over the course of a few weeks, she put the sales staff through a couple of full-day team retreats. She seemed to be winning the confidence and trust of Galaxy's team members, not only in her own department, but throughout the organization. Communication in the Marketing department was better. People seemed happy again and wanted to be there. Although many members of Marketing had initially been skeptical about this young, new manager, the employee-engagement scores seemed to be slowly moving up. It was a pretty good trend, and every month you had shared more good news with your boss and the rest of the leadership team. Three months in, everyone felt euphoric. But you knew that Lee couldn't do this job alone over the long term. Lee would need a solid leadership team that would support her ideas and give her the resources she'd need to position Galaxy for future growth.

You settle deeper into your chair and contemplate the full situation. You realize that this is like Dickens' Tale of Two Cities: "It was the best of times; it was the worst of times...." After Lee had been on the job for four months, it dawned on you that something wasn't quite right. You began to get the distinct feeling that Lee was becoming too hands-on. By the end of the fifth month, you realized that Lee wasn't delegating or coaching her team members to pick up some of her technical load. At first, you weren't overly concerned that Lee wasn't coming forward with a vision for the future. You didn't raise the issue with the leadership team because, at that point, they were hungry for any good news coming out of Marketing. No one was asking you questions about Lee's long-term plan. But you knew in your heart that Lee was becoming an operational firefighter. She was getting caught up in the day-to-day routine, and she had become more reactive than proactive.

After Lee had been doing the job for six months, you knew she had succumbed to the grind instead of becoming an opportunity-seeker and a shaper of the future. You realized that Lee needed simple, constructive feedback and encouragement, as well as coaching to help her think more broadly and allocate some time to defining her strategy for the future.

Your thoughts are suddenly interrupted by a knock at the door. Another group needs the break room, which is good timing. You can go grab an early lunch and make a few more preparations for the afternoon meeting.

As you sit in your office, relaxing and eating your favorite midday meal—a chicken-salad sandwich on rye—you ask yourself where you had gone wrong with Lee. You clearly remember having at least three focused, nice-and-easy coaching conversations in which you had clearly communicated with Lee about her strengths and opportunities for improvement. You are pretty sure you gave Lee clear and understandable feedback on her fire-fighting efforts: that they were greatly appreciated, and that everyone was ecstatic that she had made so much progress on some very difficult problems, but that it was time for her to make a strategic contribution to the business. You thought that your assignment to Lee—that she come forward with a proposal and vision of how she wanted to prepare Marketing to better handle future opportunities and challenges—had been crystal clear. You told Lee that she needed to articulate a plan for taking Zarium to the global market. Lee, in good faith, said she would think about it and get back to you. For a while, you thought everything was coming along as planned. You thought you had gotten through to her. But then weeks passed, and nothing tangible happened. She offered no ideas, even though you broached this topic on two or three other occasions and spoke about the value of strategic planning in your own team meetings.

As you consider the approach you have used with Lee, you recall the prior training and practice that has helped you develop a very good, straightforward framework for coaching and sharing feedback with others. Your approach in conversations focuses on providing genuine support and recognition, as well as a clear definition of operational and strategic expectations. Additionally, you ensure that the same approach is used with your own team leaders in Sales, Marketing, and Advertising during team meetings. So why hasn't it worked with Lee?

Frankly, you don't understand why you should have to clarify your expectations any further. As a senior manager, Lee should understand that she needs to figure out a way to produce results today and chart a course of action for the future. She needs to differentiate Galaxy by coming up with new ways to penetrate the market and to reach the customer. Unfortunately, Lee is caught in the activity trap, and you know it.

You have always thought of it as the "task magnet," the day-to-day responsibilities that grab a person's attention and hold it captive. If people fail to discipline themselves and shake free of its grip, they can't ever get ahead of the curve. This is "the tyranny of the urgent." Individuals have to be strong strategic leaders in order to stop spending all their time being doers and fixers. The crucial activities of a strategic leader are creating strategic direction and establishing priorities, communicating those ideas to other leaders in the organization, lining up resources,

and getting direct reports and senior leaders to buy in to the strategic plan.

You realize that the future is coming at Galaxy pretty fast. There is a lot of volatility in the industry, as well as competition for talent. Everyone is looking at emerging markets to find new opportunities to expand. And Galaxy definitely needs to grow, but it won't be able to reach that goal unless Marketing leads the charge. This is perfectly clear in your mind, and you feel that it should be perfectly clear in Lee's mind, too. Lee seemed to acknowledge your well-intended coaching and feedback on this issue, and she said she would work on it. You trusted that she would come through on her promise.

Just then, the alarm on your cell phone trills and interrupts your thoughts. The leadership-team meeting will convene in about an hour. You have no doubt that the team is going to ask you what you are planning to do. People are getting impatient, and Lee's time is running out. The leaders in the organization have come to realize that Lee is a problem solver, first and foremost, and you are trying to figure out how to explain the situation to them. You know that some team members will probably say that Lee isn't doing her job and needs to go. People are going to be very direct, asking you questions like, "What have you said to Lee?" "Did we make the wrong choice?" and "Can Lee be saved?" These are the same questions that have been on your mind since early this morning.

With the little time you have left before your meeting, you decide to make a call to one of your trusted mentors, a recently retired former colleague named Taylor. Taylor helped shape your career and you feel he may be able to provide advice on how to deal with Lee, your boss, and your peers. You are hoping that Taylor will have words of wisdom to share and that he will be able to give you some hope and a few new ideas. At this point, you feel you are nearing the end of your rope with Lee and have nothing to lose. Talking to Taylor about these issues certainly couldn't hurt.

CHAPTER

THREE

The Obstacles

fter you leave a couple of urgent messages, Taylor finally calls you back. Maybe this will be your lucky day after all! You and he have periodically gotten together for "lunch and learn" meetings, and it turns out that he remembers Lee from some of your previous conversations. Taylor has the ability to capture the essence of most situations rather quickly, and after you bring him up to speed on the latest developments at Galaxy and your troubles with Lee, he easily identifies what is really going on and shares his assessment of the situation.

Taylor's perspective is that you haven't used candor to have an in-depth courageous conversation with Lee yet, even though it has been discussed. He argues that while you may have discussed the subject with Lee, you have never had a heart-to-heart, eyeball-to-eyeball deep dive into your concern—and that isn't Lee's fault.

At first you are taken aback. You think that if you've had a formal discussion with someone, they should be able to pick up the message by reading between the lines and deciphering what you are really saying. Taylor understands your point but holds his ground, saying, "I need you to listen to me and consider what I say carefully. Many smart, hardworking managers, who have the very best intentions, often ignore, avoid, or withdraw from difficult situations where a deep coaching conversation is desperately needed."

Taylor's candor is admirable, a quality you have always appreciated, but you protest, claiming that you have been giving Lee feedback. Taylor pushes ahead, saying, "I understand that, but you are only touching the surface, and it seems you speed through the conversation. You haven't wrestled with the important issues underlying the symptoms." He coaches you a little more and says, "Adrian, just be patient and listen to my thoughts. You don't have to accept them, but I want you to really think about what I'm saying." He continues, "Many managers like you want to raise an issue or speak their mind, but at the same time, you struggle because you don't want to polarize the conversation or make it uncomfortable. You don't want to be labeled a troublemaker or a non-team player. This is problem number one. I'll talk about problem number two at a later time because I think that concentrating on this issue first will really help you."

"You're right, Taylor, I don't like being the bad guy and I feel that, as a manager, I should be able to say what I

need to say and move on. Anything more than that feels like overkill."

You can hear Taylor smiling through the phone as he says, "Look, I get it. I know that these conversations can create stress, consume time, and be very irritating. But without having that bold, necessary conversation with Lee, you're doing a disservice to her, to yourself, and to the organization." His assertion is simple: you haven't had an honest conversation with Lee about your expectations for her. "Whenever we leave the village of the familiar and move into new, riskier territory, we inevitably have to confront the unwelcome realities of the new terrain. And when these new realities are unpleasant, we work hard to avoid dealing with them rather than gathering the courage to have a deeper conversation. This pattern of avoidance often goes deeper than we'd like to admit. What it comes down to now, Adrian, is that you're in the process of discovering some unpleasant facts about this exciting new member of your team."

At first you fight Taylor's logic. You explain that you have been open and up front. But Taylor knows what you are up to and replies, "This tendency is really common. Many managers have an inclination to shy away from deep conversations that desperately need to happen if a business is going to succeed long term. Just like you, these managers are aware that things need to change inside their team, but they still shy away from confronting the problem directly. It's normal and acceptable to try the easy, less-risky conversation first to see if the other party will catch your drift. These managers don't want to be too provocative if it isn't really necessary. They don't want to risk agitating the other person, especially if the situation isn't that important. In the spirit of fairness and practicality, they communicate with innuendoes. They drop hints and try not to be too intense. But all too often, Adrian, speaking to surface issues just isn't enough, no matter how many times you go over them. There is no substitute for a rich, deep conversation. This is the only way to ensure a meeting of the minds and determine whether the other party can or will be able to address the issues."

Taylor pauses to allow these ideas to sink in, and then goes on, saying, "Look, the time you have left before your upcoming meeting is short. Do you have just a couple of minutes so I can expand on the first obstacle many managers face?" You look at the time and ask him to continue.

"When managers come across a situation that clearly merits deeper discussion, where full disclosure is needed and all the cards need to be put on the table, many of them get uncomfortable. You are not alone in feeling this way. When these difficult situations don't go our way, we feel uneasy, anxious, and uncertain about the outcomes. We have a subconscious fear of discovering the harsh reality the truth will create for us. In your case, when you are in doubt and unsure, you have a tendency to hold off, waiting to do the deeper dive until you have no other choice. When you approach an issue this way, you end up skimming the surface and gingerly approaching the topic, even though a deeper dive is clearly needed. These feelings are natural, but they cause leaders to become preoccupied with not wanting to hurt or offend people or to blow the issue out of proportion. Most good leaders find themselves in situations where they talk themselves out of having deeper, sometimes high-stakes, conversations that need to happen for the benefit of the whole organization." You let Taylor know you understand what he means. You've experienced managers who react the way he is describing.

"But, I guess I don't see myself that way. I think I'm pretty straight forward and open most of the time. Are you saying you have observed me avoiding issues?"

"Well, Adrian, the answer is 'yes.' We've known each other for a long time and I know you are an effective and competent manager, but in order to move forward, I think you have to have a courageous conversation with yourself. You have to honestly explore your intentions and examine who you are protecting—and all too often, managers are only protecting themselves. Sometimes, they try to cover up the fact that they don't feel completely confident or competent about their skills to orchestrate a potentially painful, yet productive, conversation. And sometimes these managers hesitate because they worry that they won't manage their own emotions well if the topic gets heated or if the other person gets upset. My sense is this is happening to you.

"Adrian, we can't control how others choose to respond to the discussion, but what we can control is our own courage and willingness to overcome our fears about initiating a conversation. You'll need to have a serious and rational discussion with yourself as to whether you should move forward into deeper water or stay where you are. After weighing the risks against the rewards, you may decide to just let it go. While you may never become eager to engage others in tough, candid conversations or enthusiastic about confronting complex or sensitive problems that come up in business, you can develop the ability to work through your own discomfort and your perception of the dangers related to opening a robust discussion about the crucial issues you're facing."

You take a moment to clarify what Taylor is saying. "So you think I need to assess my own willingness to

have a difficult conversation, and what my motives are, before I approach the subject? That sounds like a lot of self-evaluation and I don't have much time before my meeting. What do you suggest for today?"

"Look, Adrian, I know you have to run. But before you go, I'd like you to think about something for a moment: You have to accept the fact that the timing is never ideal and there's never a perfect place to start moving forward and broaching these challenging conversations. But if you are willing to go to a place that is uncomfortable, these tough dilemmas can make a difference in the lives of people, allowing them to grow and the organization to flourish.

"Your job today is just to get through the meeting with your boss and peers. Make a commitment to find the answers they seek and to report back to them. Let your colleagues know you're interested in their ideas. Be accountable and own up to the fact that you need to work with Lee on a much deeper level to discover her capabilities—and her limitations. And when you've finished with your meeting and you've had a chance to think, let's talk again. Maybe on your commute home? Give me a call when you're ready."

You thank Taylor and slowly hang up the phone. Wow, he certainly had a lot to say about how to approach difficult conversations. You always appreciate his insight, but this time you think he may have missed the mark. You sincerely think you communicated your expectations to Lee clearly and often, but you just aren't getting the results you anticipated. Now it's time to face the senior management team and you feel your stress level rising. You shake your head and, feeling more than a little confused, you shift your attention to preparing for the meeting.

＊ ＊ ＊ ＊ ＊ ＊ ＊

You enter the large conference room and gaze out at the cityscape. Everyone is gathering, talking animatedly, clearly motivated by a few breakthroughs the organization is experiencing. The energy in the room is palpable. The meeting is called to order and the first order of business is presented: the Marketing department. Unfortunately, the sense of excitement is quickly eclipsed by the mere mention of the Marketing department. Just as you had anticipated, the group is keenly aware that while the Marketing department is great at knocking down operational grease fires, Lee is not preparing the department for the future. Several of them concur that as far as they can tell, she simply doesn't have either a long-term vision or a departmental strategy that will support the organization's overarching priorities. The consensus of the group is that Lee is getting good at working "in the business" but not "on the business," and that without the Marketing department helping to leverage the company's competitive advantages and differentiate Galaxy in a changing industry, Galaxy will always struggle to be a legitimate player in the market.

Your colleagues on the leadership team are anxious to find out what you have already said to Lee about her strategic role in the company. You are quick to assure them that from an operational standpoint, Lee has things well on track; you also try to ease their minds by telling them that you have had several conversations with her where you coached her and encouraged her to make a plan to shape the long-term direction of the department. But you can tell that your explanations aren't doing anything to satisfy the misgivings that many of these leaders still have about Lee. They shift in their chairs and seem to have a lot of questions. You know they are probably wondering if you have done enough in-depth coaching with Lee; if so, maybe Lee just isn't up to the task.

The Vice President of Human Resources is the only person to say what is clearly on everyone's mind: "Is it worth trying to do more with Lee, or is it time to move on? She really doesn't seem to be getting the message." This question makes you flash back to your conversation with Taylor, and you wonder if he might actually be right. Have you really used enough candor to have a courageous conversation with Lee about the gaps in her performance, or have you just been hoping that she would catch your drift without you actually laying it all out on the line?

You decide to follow Taylor's advice about today's meeting, and you tell the group that you appreciate the question and that you have also thought about these issues. You explain that you agree that Lee has been successful in getting the department back on track from an operational point of view, but you think that you may now need to have a deeper conversation with her about Galaxy's strategic expectations of her—and her department—and find out for certain whether she's ready and willing to take on the role of a truly strategic leader. You know that you owe it to Lee and to the organization as a whole to have this conversation with her before you decide to officially pull the plug on Lee's career at Galaxy. This answer seems to satisfy the group's immediate questions, but the team's patience is clearly waning—including yours, and it's your responsibility to help Lee get on a forward-looking track—or she'll be out of a job. You have no time to spare. You know for certain now that you've got to get things on the right track.

FOUR

Denial

You head back to your office after your leadership meeting ends. The conversation you'd had with Taylor earlier in the day starts running through your mind. When you got off the phone with him, you were pretty frustrated and decided that he doesn't have a good sense of what is really going on. You've always considered yourself to be pretty courageous. Nothing about business really scares you. You again push his words to the back of your mind and go to work putting out your own fires and finishing up your day.

You arrive home, after the usual brain-jostling train ride. You take lettuce, tomato, cucumber, and a leftover chicken breast out of the refrigerator and begin making a salad. What happened in the meeting and Taylor's words are running through your head as you slice each vegetable.

You don't like what Taylor said, but your approach hasn't been working, has it? What if Taylor is on to something? His message suddenly begins to make sense. You lean back against the counter and admit to yourself that, although your intentions have been good, Taylor is right: You have been in denial about what has been motivating your actions.

At first, you rationalized your behavior by convincing yourself that you were protecting Lee. You just didn't want to hurt her feelings, you told yourself, and making a deeper dive into the issue might do just that. You rationalized that she should be smart enough to connect the dots. And, quite candidly, you didn't want to derail her progress. After all, she was making positive strides and doing one half of her job very successfully. Even your boss and colleagues noticed the progress Lee was making with putting out Marketing's fires, and they had provided you with great feedback for the first three, four, even five months of Lee's employment. People noticed the difference across the whole organization.

However, the bigger, long-term challenges were still buried underground—and you were hoping that Lee would be able to figure them out on her own. You didn't want to have to give her strict instructions. You wanted Lee to effortlessly blossom into the kind of person you really needed in that job. Your self-deception went so deep that you had yourself fully convinced that your failure to candidly talk with Lee had been all about her.

But the more you reflect on the situation, the more you realize that the person you were really protecting was yourself. You weren't managing your own fears well at all. Your uneasiness and sense of risk had slyly enticed you into this approach-avoidance trap, and Lee's future with the organization was in jeopardy because of it. On one hand, you wanted to courageously confront the issues with Lee. On the other hand, you recognized that she was unable (or unwilling) to create a strategic plan for her department. Even with that recognition, however, when it came time to speak frankly about this issue, you had soft-peddled the message.

You encouraged her to try, but you didn't make it clear that coming up with a strategic plan for the Marketing department was a requirement—a mandate that had the potential to end Lee's career at Galaxy if it wasn't taken seriously. Frankly, you were afraid to deliver that message clearly because it was uncomfortable for you. Imagining a future without Lee made you extremely uneasy. You had become attached to her, and you'd convinced yourself that you could save her, so you denied her the opportunity to hear the message honestly. In the process, you had also denied yourself the opportunity to hone your skills, wrestle with your demons, and work through your internal resistance, hesitation, fear, and apprehension. You put all of the salad ingredients in a bowl and pour on a generous portion of blue cheese dressing. Wow! This is a bit of an "aha" moment for you, a tough-minded manager who thought you knew yourself and weren't afraid of anything.

After another busy morning at the office, and you make a commitment to take the issue head on. You think about it carefully, and you conclude that there is nothing about this situation that you can't handle. You will tell Lee the honest, unvarnished truth; you'll lay everything out on the table and explain your concern to Lee in a much more direct way. You aren't worried any more. You have pondered the message over the course of the night, and you have this under control. You are confident about your approach, so you call and schedule an afternoon meeting with Lee. You are looking forward to this meeting, as you have tamed your fears and did so pretty easily, in fact.

When you meet with Lee, you really lay it on the line for her, and you are sure that she got the message this time. Your tone is firm, emphatic, demanding—and rightfully so! You are in and out in record time; the whole conversation takes a grand total of ten minutes. You are so pleased with your performance that you immediately call Taylor to proudly give him your report.

As luck would have it, Taylor is cooling his heels after playing a morning round of golf with his buddies and jumps right on the call. Taylor loves people and loves developing people, and he's always gracious with his time. As soon as he answers, he asks, "What's the report?" You eagerly and enthusiastically reply, "I did it! Our conversation was short and sweet. I cut right to the bone. I laid it all out there, and now Lee knows she can either do what I say or move on."

You go on for twenty minutes describing your ten-minute conversation because you are so excited. You run out of breath and realize that you haven't let Taylor get a single word in, so you ask him what he thinks. Does he think Lee gets it now? The line is quiet for so long that you think the call dropped. You ask Taylor if you lost him.

He slowly, deliberately, and with significant courage, quietly says, "Adrian, I think you blew it."

You retort, "What do you mean, 'you blew it'? I did exactly what you suggested. I confronted Lee with the bare truth. I cut right to the chase and didn't mince words with her. I did everything I was supposed to do!"

In his typical, calm way, Taylor simply says, "I hear you. But here's my fear: I'm worried that you made mistake number two."

Now you are getting angry, and your frustration comes through in your voice, "Jeez, Taylor, how many mistakes are out there? What it really comes down to is that at the end of the day, business is business, and if Lee can't take it straight, then she shouldn't be a manager."

Taylor pauses, as he typically does before he answers, and then begins again. "Straight talk is good, but we may be talking about something else in this situation. Mistake number two is very, very common. Let me describe it to you, and you can tell me whether the shoe fits: When you've been nibbling around the edges of a big issue for a while—talking but not getting to the core—frustration, disappointment, and irritation often build up. Sometimes these emotions become so strong that when you finally have a candid conversation, you move immediately into a position where you're trying to win at any cost. Sometimes you may even attack the person outright. My fear is that you went from nibbling at the edges right into the attack mode. Forgive me for saying it this way, but it seems like you ended up wanting to punish her. In your mind, the conversation seemed short and sweet: strike and get out in ten minutes or less. But my guess is that Lee was completely broadsided and left your meeting in a state of shock."

You still feel like you were in the right in terms of the way you'd handled the conversation, and you aren't shy about sharing your opinion with Taylor. You tell him,

"Shock? That sounds good to me, Taylor. I wanted to shock her."

"I hear you," Taylor replies. "But from the way you're describing it, from your tone, and from what I have learned by watching other managers in the past, the conversation you had with her went beyond shocking her. You went in for the kill."

You are flabbergasted. You question Taylor, "Are you serious? Do you think I killed Lee's spirit, drive, and passion for the job?" Breaking Lee hadn't been your intention at all. You just wanted her to take your request more seriously.

Thoughtfully, Taylor says, "I don't know the dynamics of your relationship with Lee as well as you do, but I do think you've done some harm. She may still love the work and love her team, but you've beaten her down. As a result, she may cower around you now, much like an animal who's been hurt by its master. I don't mind you being tough, honest, and direct. But she may have seen this as a flash flood, a torrent of rage rushing towards her, and in that situation, all she could think to do was scramble to get out of that ten-minute meeting as fast as she could."

You pause for a minute and tell Taylor that you need to think. Taylor is understanding and says, "No problem. I know it will take some time for you to absorb everything we're talking about. Approaching a candid conversation in the way you did is a classic number-two mistake. The pendulum swings from working on the edge of the issue to overwhelming people with your truth and candor, to the point where you're so zealous about it that you can't stop yourself. In police work, they call it 'post-pursuit syndrome.'"

You wonder out loud, "Post-pursuit syndrome? What's that?"

He explains, "Well, when you are agitated and in pursuit of a perpetrator, when you finally catch up with your subject, you want to beat that person to a pulp. Whenever people are impatient and passionate about achieving an important goal, this same scenario plays out. You're eager to get Galaxy to the next level by effectively marketing great new products, and you're eager to have a perfect person in that role. Because you're so committed to Galaxy's success, you feel like you have to take control of the situation, and if people are standing in your way, you'll take them down. This is classic post-pursuit behavior. You overreacted and really took Lee to task, to the point where she probably feels beaten and like there's no way to win. If that is the case, she'll hunker down and withdraw. She'll go into survival mode. She's probably hoping that you were just having a bad day and that she happened to be standing in the crossfire during this brief, but brutal, conversation. This is just a theory. But give it some thought. You always know how to reach me."

You respond, "Yeah, I do. Thanks Taylor. I will think about what you've said." Stunned, you end the call. You feel awful. You honestly thought Taylor would be so proud of your work. You can't think about this right now. It is taking too much of your time and energy, and you are confused and need to take a deep breath. You were feeling ecstatically proud of your willingness to face your fears and now you feel lower than low—all in a matter of minutes. What if you blew your opportunity to bring Lee around and let her skills flourish? You know now you likely stomped on the tender shoots of a strategic flower, and you are so disappointed in yourself. But maybe Taylor had gotten it all wrong. *Hey*, you tell yourself, *business is business. They have got to learn to deal with it.* You decide to just wait and see. Maybe Taylor really is off base. After all, he wasn't there and hadn't actually heard you deliver the message.

CHAPTER
FIVE

Lee's Response

A fter a tumultuous week, you feel fortunate to have a glorious weekend ahead of you. Time spent outdoors with friends and family does wonders for your mood and rejuvenates your spirit. As you head to work early Monday morning, you find that you are still processing Taylor's bold feedback. Once you arrive at your desk, however, you experience a surprising turn of events. There, on your keyboard, is a little note from Lee, which simply says, "I have something important to share with you, and I need to see you at your earliest convenience."

Wow! This is unexpected. You think to yourself, *I didn't see that one coming. I wonder what's on Lee's mind. Has she decided to abandon ship? Is she angry at me? Or is it something simple, like a question about her budget or someone she'd like to hire?* Rather than thinking about it all day, you send Lee a quick text message that says, "Hey, I'm available now. Let's meet in the small conference room. We can talk as long as you want." Lee responds, "I'll see you in five."

You enter the small conference room, where Lee is waiting. She is very cordial but gets right to the point, "Adrian, I've been thinking about our last conversation for the last several days and, I must say, I am still a little shaken."

You gently reply, "I can understand that. Go ahead; tell me more."

"Well, when I first got here, everyone was pretty explicit about all of the problems that needed to be fixed. Quite honestly, I intentionally focused really hard on resolving them, and I think I have been very successful. However, it seemed like the more I worked, the more problems I uncovered, and every one of them needed my urgent attention. Would you agree?"

You nod, saying, "No question about it. We had to dig our way out of a mountain of messes that had been growing for two or three years."

Lee looks at you and continues. "Well, Adrian, I feel like everyone recognized my efforts, and I appreciate that. And yes, I heard you talk about long-term strategies; at our team meeting, you mentioned having a vision and creating a strategic agenda to share with others. Then, I heard you and others talking about that at our quarterly all-management conferences. But frankly, I didn't see anyone else taking the issue seriously. I haven't even seen a draft or proposal on a strategic vision from you. I haven't received any tools, training, or guidance on how to formulate strategy as a manager in the middle of the organization. Adrian, this isn't an accusation, but I haven't seen anything from senior management either. Oh, I got the usual new-employee orientation packet; I see the annual reports; I overhear conversations. But what I don't see is a coherent message from senior leadership about our strategic intentions as a company and where we want to be in five or ten years. As a result, I've been a little confused about whether investing my energy and time in strategy formulation is a real expectation you have of me or whether it's nothing but talk."

For a moment you imagine taking Lee by the shoulders and shaking some sense into her. You restrain yourself, swallow the sharp retort sitting on the tip of your tongue, and state calmly, "There's probably some truth to what you are saying, Lee, and I am trying to see the situation from your perspective."

But then Lee unexpectedly shifts the conversation. She says, "All that aside, the thing that has bothered me the most over the last few days is the way this whole issue is being handled."

"What do you mean?" you ask. "I've just been trying to broach the issues candidly so that we can have an adult conversation about some things that have been on my mind."

Lee responds quickly, saying "No, I get that. Let me just try to explain how it looked to me. For probably six or seven months, I felt like creating this forward-looking, long-term plan was positioned as a rather low-priority issue for me, something that I would have more time to worry about after I'd made some progress with all of the tactical fires that needed to be put out. Then, last week, you seemed to come at me out of the blue, and I felt ambushed. In the course of ten wild minutes, you beat me into the ground over this issue. I was left trying to make sense out of this dramatic swing from relatively low priority to something completely off the charts.

"Adrian, over the last several months I have felt that you haven't been very well informed about what I'd been thinking or what I've been doing in the strategic space. Let me just share with you the way I see it: When you chewed me out last week, it seemed like you really hadn't done your homework. You made a lot of assumptions about what I have and haven't done. I love the idea of running this business from a more strategic point of view, and I actually do have an outline of my strategic objectives for the next three years. It's not terribly detailed, but it does exist. Where I'm getting stuck is on answering specific questions: How fast do we want to move? Where will my resources come from? In what ways do my strategic objectives align with those of other functional areas or senior leaders?

"Last week, it felt to me like you had made a choice: to attack my intentions and my character. You had decided that you had to win this argument, even though no argument existed. But you made those decisions about my performance without having good data. You bulldozed right over me without having all the facts, thinking through what you were going to say, or conducting the conversation in a rational way." After letting this sink in for a moment, Lee adds, "I just have two other quick points to make, and then I'll get out of your hair.

"I believe that in order to build a successful relationship with you and other members of the senior-management team here at Galaxy, I need a shared commitment to working through our future plan together. For the last six or seven months, commitment to this strategy initiative has been very low, and then last week, your intensity about its importance was off the scale. In the future, we both need to better communicate our personal commitment to leading strategic, long-term change at Galaxy. Our dedication to this company's strategic growth can't run from cold to hot.

"That's why I was a little defensive last week. It seemed like you had made a unilateral decision that starting right that minute, we were all going to become more proactive in the way we run the business. Without any input from me, and without even asking if I had anything to say, you decided that I'd failed in my role. I haven't failed at all. I just think there are a few things we have to consider and some tradeoffs we need to keep in mind if you want me to shift my focus to more serious strategic work—which, by the way, I can easily do. But instead of an edict, I need this to be a collaborative process."

Lee pauses for a moment and then says, "That's all I have. I don't mean to sound disrespectful or noncompliant. That's not my intention at all. It's just that this quick shift in your mindset gave me a little mental whiplash. I realize that I may have missed the signals. It's clear to me now that I didn't pick up on the subtle messages you were sending earlier this year. But here's the thing, Adrian: I am not good at deciphering hints. I need clarity, I need specificity, and I need openness—but that level of candor can't feel like an assault. When people attack me because they don't have all the facts, or when they fail to keep their emotions in check, I get really demotivated. I value a leader who allows some give and take, someone who checks with me to see if I agree that a given topic is timely, important, and worthy of a heavy conversation. I need a leader who is willing to brainstorm and collaborate with me. When somebody doesn't seem willing to help with the problem-solving or decision-making process, it really frustrates me.

"I spent a lot of time thinking about this over the weekend, and a lot of energy asking myself whether Galaxy—and the relationship I have with you, Adrian—is really going to work for me. But after a long time, I came to the conclusion that I want it to work. I think you and I could have great chemistry, and I want to be part of the future space that Galaxy could occupy. I know that Marketing has to make dramatic changes to the way we do business in the months and years ahead. If we don't, we will become irrelevant. I know Galaxy could go to the open market and buy a lot of the services that we are currently providing internally, like marketing. I can see that I have competition out there. Other functions and groups inside Galaxy are in the same situation; they'll have to change as well. I don't mind trying something new and being asked to create my own strategy inside the business. I just need a lot of guidance, input, and reassurance—and less of the emotional intensity I felt from you last week.

"Adrian, I need you to know that I respect you, and if you want to think about what I've said and let me know what you think, that would be great. If you want to talk about strategy or anything else, I'm available any time this week. I know that you have a big meeting this afternoon, and I suspect you'll talk about this and a lot of other things that are going on inside Galaxy. But as soon as it's convenient for you, I'd like to follow up with you. I

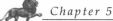

appreciate you taking a few moments to listen to me this morning. I hope your meeting goes well." Lee turns and walks through the door.

Lee certainly said what was on her mind. As you process what she had said, you think to yourself that you wouldn't be a bit surprised if she had already updated her resume. Who knows? Maybe she had even made a call to Michael, the headhunter who had lined her up with Galaxy in the first place, to inform him that she was back out on the market. But in your heart of hearts, you truly believe what she said this morning. Everyone has made some mistakes, and if you commit to working together, you might just be able to get this going in the right direction. You appreciate the spirit of her conversation and admit, with some embarrassment, that she had done a much better job with her ten minutes of conversation than you had with yours.

Though you want to further mull over your conversation with Lee, you have to switch gears. There is still a lot of material to prepare for the meeting this afternoon, and you need all the time you can get. You resolve to work on your interactions with Lee during your commute home. Perhaps you can impose on Taylor yet again. You feel confident that he will help you make some sense out of these events. You know that you are moving forward and are feeling pretty good about your progress, despite your tendency to avoid confrontation and your apparently hostile response of late. You hope to be strong enough to fight through this situation and your personal shortcomings—and that you'll ultimately have Lee in your corner. You knew she could grow into a great asset for Galaxy, and in hindsight, you have to admit that she did some excellent coaching with you this morning and made some very good points. You have a lot to think about over the next few days.

SIX

Minimizing and Winning In Depth

Whenever you get a little stressed or over-wrought, it helps you to go running. You like to run. You ran competitive track and field in high school, and during your college years, you ran to alleviate academic stress. Once you entered the professional world, you continued to use running as a therapeutic, invigorating way to clear your mind when things got crazy at work. Though you've been a runner throughout your career, you don't get a chance to run every day; your workload and managerial demands simply don't afford you that freedom. But if you can get out a couple of times a week, it really does do wonderful things for your mind.

You run this morning out of sheer necessity. You've felt out of control all week, like you were heading straight for a mental train wreck. With your legs pumping and your breath coming fast and hard in the damp morning air, you are able to think more clearly. Today is no exception, though the weather isn't ideal. A light rain drizzles and the chill bites through your warm-up jacket. After 45 minutes you head home.

You step through the door and head right for your mobile phone. You need some clarification. In trying to understand yourself and the situation better, you want to know why Taylor thinks you are still missing the mark with Lee. Not wanting to bother him with a call too early in the morning, you send Taylor a text message to see if he is willing to meet you for lunch this afternoon at a great local sushi restaurant. You know that Taylor loves sushi. If you are willing to buy him lunch, how can he pass it up?

Taylor gets back to you almost immediately, saying he'd love to have lunch with you, but he can't do it until tomorrow. Although you try not to be too disappointed, your pessimism gets the better of you and you think, *Oh, great. Another day living with this uncertainty—I can hardly wait.* But given the circumstances, you know that being patient is your only option. At least the meeting is set.

The next day, you arrive at the sushi bar and wait patiently for an opportunity to talk about Lee. Taylor senses that you have a lot on your mind, and when he inquires about Lee, you see your chance to lay it all out there. Putting your pride aside, you tell Taylor about how Lee confronted you. You explain that she was bothered by the way you had been handling the situation and felt blindsided by the shift in focus and expectations. You lean in a little and confide your concern, "I wouldn't be surprised if Lee decides she needs to move on, but my

gut tells me that she genuinely wants to re-commit and try to make it work. She was seeking my help and input, but clearly would like me to be less intense." You finish relating all of the details of Lee's response to your demand for a strategic plan.

Taylor thinks while he finishes another savory bite of his spider roll. "Adrian, it seems to me that Lee's willingness to share what was on her mind is a good sign—a signal that she thinks there is an opportunity to collaborate and that she is truly interested in understanding your expectations, as well as those of senior management, regarding the Marketing department. I think it's great that she shared her perspective with you. I can tell you've given it some thought."

You nod, saying, "Taylor, I want to thank you for your guidance. But quite frankly, I'm really confused. I hope you can help me understand exactly what I need to do. Could you please just start again at the beginning? I'll listen carefully to everything you say. I feel like I have to address this leadership gap if I'm going to be fully effective in my role. My conversations with you have raised my awareness about my need to improve my communication skills. I know I need to be candid and clear, but I sense that I'm not doing it the best way I can."

Taylor sits back, "Fair enough. I'll summarize what I've been trying to convey, and we'll see if that clears up your confusion. Your intentions are good, Adrian. Your desired outcomes are clear and perfectly legitimate. It's obvious to me that you really want the best for the company, for its employees, for Lee, and for yourself.

"Good relationships and good performance begin with clear, positive interactions and honest communication.

Open communication leads to understanding—understanding about what Lee wants and what you want. When people communicate clearly with one another and receive candid feedback, they can make the choices that are best for them: choices to step up, to step out, or to change the situation. In any case, they can make educated choices. Honest communication also leads to respect—maybe not friendship, but respect. And respect is crucial in any organization. Ultimately, respect leads to trust. When trust is present in the organization, everyone relaxes. Team members feel confident that they can rely on their colleagues to champion and support them. You won't always agree. You may even experience some painful, heated conflict. But when people operate with full disclosure and full understanding, interactions of all types—including confrontation—are that much more constructive. I think that in your case, the first step in the process of creating a high-performance organization has been missing in your conversations with Lee."

"But, I feel I have been open and honest with Lee, so why isn't it working?"

"More often than not, when a conversation or a relationship isn't progressing the way you had hoped or expected, you tend to form what's called a 'self-serving bias.' Your self-serving bias suggests that when things aren't going as you'd planned, the other party is to blame. On the flip side, when things are going well, you tend to attribute the success to your own effort and skill, while ignoring the contributions that others may have made to the positive situation. It takes a pretty astute manager to have the presence of mind to step back, look at the situation honestly, and ask, 'What am I contributing to this communication that is helping it to be effective? What part am I playing if this communication is ineffective?' Managers need to take a very high level of personal responsibility for their own effectiveness first; and for a lot of managers with big egos, degrees from top-tier schools, and a track record of overconfidence, becoming acutely aware of their own weaknesses can be painful. I like to refer to these blind spots as 'the curse of the brilliant.' You've been very successful in your career, Adrian. But the problem is that the smarter you are, and the more successful you have been, the harder it is to see your own self-serving biases."

You think about how you might have employed this "self-serving bias" as you savor another piece of sushi and Taylor sips his tea. You can see he is letting his words sink in.

"Taylor, I appreciate your insight, but how do I avoid this bias?"

Taylor continues, "As I mentioned to you before, I think you have fallen into some traps in your recent conversations with Lee. These traps are rooted in the natural tendencies and instincts you require as a human being to remain comfortable and safe or to establish dominance over your rivals. The former is reflected in your desire to 'minimize.' Do you remember what we talked about in our first conversation about Lee? How you naturally want to make the workplace comfortable and your conversations pleasant? You want to lessen the tension and minimize any bad feelings you sense in the relationship or during a critical conversation with a person who matters to you in some way. You want to avoid upsetting Lee. The result is that you inadvertently end up setting yourself up for failure, which makes you less productive, less comfortable, and more irritable. In your desire not to offend Lee or put her on the defensive, you've become a subconscious minimizer. Look, Adrian, this has happened to me more times in my career than I can count. I just wish I had been more aware of it sooner, so being able to help you by sharing my perspective is a really great opportunity. I just hope that what I have to say will benefit you."

You nod and, urging him on, you say, "Taylor, I am really interested in what you have said so far and curious about what you are going to say next."

"Adrian, from what you have shared with me to this point, it seems like you start these difficult conversations by asking a lot of questions instead of coming right out and immediately focusing on the issue. Now, that's okay early on, especially during regular coaching and feedback sessions with your team. But when you reach a tipping point in the relationship and it's time to dive into a deep conversation, asking a lot of questions could feel manipulative to the person on the receiving end. On the surface, open-ended questions appear to be harmless. From your perspective, they probably sound completely sincere and non-threatening. But when Lee fails to catch your meaning and doesn't answer these questions in a way that satisfies you, like many of us, you may default to a more direct line of questioning. And with closed-ended questions, you too often end up with thin, closed responses.

"Let's think about a typical scenario. You open your conversation with Lee in the way that's most comfortable for you—avoiding confronting the hard issues head on by asking a lot of questions. Lee gets frustrated when you make a lot of inquiries. She's probably wondering where you're going with all the questions you're asking. Maybe she gets a little defensive because she feels like she's being interrogated. And after everything else, she starts giving you one-word answers to the questions you ask. Instead of opening a dialogue, you've managed to snap it shut—and I know that's not your goal. Does this sound about right?"

You nod your head, "Taylor, I think you may be clair-voyant. That sounds really familiar."

"The truth is, Adrian, when you work your way down through a communication funnel, you'll always reach a point where the other person needs to hear your clear, straightforward interpretation of the situation at hand. The person you are talking with deserves nothing less. However, this doesn't mean that you are always right, and thinking you are can be dangerous. Knowing it all is a really heavy burden to carry, Adrian. Rather than being absolutely certain about your stand, be somewhat provisional. Say something like, 'There are a few things I need to share with you, and I hope you'll be willing to listen to what I have to say,' and then get on with sharing your thoughts. And when you do, make sure there's no edge to your voice. Avoid using harsh language and all-encompassing words like 'always' or 'must.' Make your message clear and simple.

"Getting back to Lee, I would argue that if you aren't taking the responsibility to confront the issues you see with her directly, you are asking her to take her best guess about where you're really coming from, and in these kinds of situations, the likelihood that she's going to guess wrong is quite high. At best, she'll misinterpret parts of your message, and at worst, she'll ignore you—and the issues at hand—and simply carry on as usual."

You respond, "I can see what you are saying, Taylor, but if I'm minimizing, I'm not doing it intentionally. I just want the conversation to be comfortable. In the past, I wanted Lee to see the problem without having to be so direct."

Taylor smiles. "The problem is, more often than not, that just isn't realistic. In a few, relatively uncomplicated situations, asking questions and subtly edging around the topic can work. But most of the time, this less courageous approach to conversations has a negative impact on our effectiveness as leaders, our relationships with our team members, and their ability to execute on our expectations; and we aren't even aware of it."

You think for a moment and then ask, "So, is it just the questioning technique that is off base?"

"No, not always," Taylor explains. "Most of the time, asking a few focused questions is a good thing. This is how you'll gain insight into how Lee sees the situation and what she's thinking. Providing Lee with appropriate praise is also a good thing, because it's important for her to know that you recognize the value she brings to the organization. However, sometimes this tendency to minimize comes out when you use praise excessively, and it ends up sounding patronizing. For example, if you were to shower Lee with compliments, beginning the conversation by telling her that she is coming along fine and that she is doing a good job in these areas, you will end up sending her a very mixed message, and she'll resent it. When praise is used in a difficult discussion, your intention is to make the other person feel good. But is that really your motive? I believe that using praise in a tense and potentially controversial situation is really designed

to make you, as the leader, feel less uncomfortable—not to make the other person feel good.

"Remember what I said before: Asking questions and giving people praise are both good things, but I would argue that during a challenging coaching situation or a courageous conversation like the one you've been trying to have with Lee, these approaches have the potential to do more harm than good. It's all about timing. There's a time for questions, a time for praise, and a time to get down to brass tacks. By doing what's comfortable, you either rob Lee of the opportunity to deliver results, or you rob yourself of an opportunity to understand the root cause of Lee's ineffectiveness.

"However, the need for this conversation with me indicates that you've reached a tipping point. In your last conversation with Lee, your intent was to address a crucial problem: Lee's ability to envision Galaxy's long-term direction and your expectation that she come up with strategic ideas for her area of responsibility that align with the company's goals. If that's what you want to discuss, you need to go right to that topic. The key is to avoid creating confusion. In your next conversation, Lee should not have to wonder whether the praise you give her is sincere, and she shouldn't need to ask herself whether you are trying to manipulate her, create harmony, or smooth things over. Your intentions should be crystal clear.

"Adrian, minimizing behaviors can be used to keep things cool and comfortable. Sometimes, you may even pretend to agree with Lee, using broad, ambiguous terms to talk about the situation or suggesting that this conversation is about the group rather than about Lee specifically. The problem is that playing it safe is incredibly costly to everyone because it comes at the expense of actually dealing with the issue and discovering real solutions. I believe that open, robust, courageous conversations have to be preceeded with lots of other kinds of communication. You have to be comfortable having frank conversations and conducting skillful coaching discussions. You have to know how to ask good questions and provide useful feedback so when you do reach that tipping point, you've already developed the skills and the relationship you'll need to be really honest and direct, but in a constructive way. You can get to the point without sending the wrong message or seeming like you are angry or attacking the other person. But we can talk about that topic at our next lunch if you like."

You smile and nod. "I would like to hear your ideas on that subject, but let me ask you this: I think I avoided minimizing in this last conversation with Lee—to a fault—but are you saying that I went too far the other way? That what I said may even have been destructive to my relationship with Lee?"

Taylor nods. "What I'm really talking about here is the classic fight-or-flight response. I think you were dancing around some of the things you had been seeing for months, and you inadvertently went into 'fight' mode when you approached Lee. On our last call, I heard you say that you 'flipped a switch.' You went into the conversation wanting to win. That's the fight response. You were talking about really important stuff with Lee, like charting a future course of action for the Marketing department, when you flipped that switch. What got in the way was your need to win, to be right, to sell your perspective so that Lee would see the situation the way you see it. Your approach

is a perfect example of the other natural tendency I mentioned before—the need to establish dominance and the need to win.

"When you go in wanting to win a conversation, you employ a very different set of behaviors. That's why your last conversation was only ten minutes long. Typically, win-mode conversations consist of a lot of fast talking, very little listening, and almost no inquiry. You probably laid out the facts as you see them, dismissed Lee's point of view, and used the hard-sell approach. All of these things resulted in a trade-off: You traded long-term learning and progress for the feeling that you had persuaded Lee of the rightness of your position. Unfortunately, you won short-term compliance at best, and you also gave her an out: If Lee buys your approach and things still fall apart, it's your fault. This creates another kind of tension, one that will increase distance and defensiveness in your relationship with Lee. It will also decrease the likelihood that you'll be able to solve the strategy problem you have at Galaxy." Taylor pauses for a breath and smiles.

"Adrian, I've done a lot of talking in the last hour. I truly believe that candid interactions aren't about changing the other person but are about understanding the predictable and ineffective conversation traps that we all fall into—and taking mindful steps towards changing those behaviors so we can achieve the outcomes we truly desire."

You are listening intently, without interrupting, and are humbly trying to take it all in. You take a deep breath and answer, "Taylor, this conversation was exactly what I needed, and I don't disagree with you at all. I'd like to believe that after all my training, I have finally gotten past these kinds of conversation traps, but there are clearly times when I'm not self-aware enough, and that's an area I definitely need to improve. I have to be able to understand what is going on inside my own head so I can be in a better position to convey my message about a difficult problem and facilitate a resolution that satisfies everyone involved. I have probably put too much stock in my technical training, my fact-based approach, my sense of certainty. In fact, my service in the military taught me to stay strong and convey complete self-assurance about my decisions and choices; at times, I think I just get carried away." Your brow furrows in thought.

Taylor puts your mind at ease, "It's easy to do, and we all do it. Look, Adrian, this is a lifelong battle. You are always going to be susceptible to self-deception, and it's easy to lose sight of the skills you've honed your entire life. It takes practice, discipline, and courage to speak your mind in a tactful and constructive way. It's hard to break the habit of minimizing your feelings and hinting around your concerns. But I really believe you'll be great at this. I think you can do it."

You are quick to respond. "Taylor, I don't want you to take this the wrong way, but I don't think I'm ready. I don't fully recognize the pattern, and I'm sure I don't know what kinds of skills I'll need to have. Right now, I think I approach bold discussions in a kind of piecemeal fashion, but I don't think that's the right way to do it. You seem to have a specific process or framework that you use in these kinds of situations. If you are willing to share your approach with me, I'd love to learn more about it."

Taylor says, "Well, I appreciate your honesty, Adrian. And you're right—I have developed an approach to orchestrating candid conversations that I've tried to refine over the last decade or so. I don't know that it's perfect, but I'll be glad to walk you through it. I love working with you, and if any of my suggestions help, you're welcome to use them. You'll just need to adapt them to your own communication style, culture, and background; you'll have to take those things into account when you're talking with others. I'd be glad to share any wisdom I have with you. However," he adds with a wink, "it's going to cost you another sushi lunch next week."

You smile. "Gaining a completely different approach to communication in exchange for having lunch with you seems like a really small price to pay. Where would you like to meet?"

Taylor thinks for a moment and then suggests, "The framework I'll introduce you to next week will require a pretty detailed outline. It may be easier to understand if you can see the whole process written down. Why don't we meet on Wednesday in a conference room at Galaxy and then head to lunch afterwards?"

"That sounds great," you reply. "I'll see you then!"

SEVEN

The Model

You feel like all eyes are on you right now and sense a lot of pressure to produce the forward-looking, aggressive, visionary plan that Galaxy's senior leaders expect. You understand now that the stress you've been feeling about this whole Lee situation has manifested itself in two ways: You have either denied or avoided the issue, hoping that the problem would resolve itself, or you've swung in completely the opposite direction, going into the attack mode and damaging your relationships with others in the process. You know that you can get through this, but the question that is weighing most heavily on your mind is what lies between these two extremes. What path do you need to follow? What skills do you need to do this well? How do you send a strong message without engaging in post-pursuit syndrome and breaking Lee's spirit? How do you move past

using subtle references and hints? What you really need is a handful of concrete suggestions, and you are certain that Taylor will come through for you once again.

Taylor meets you in the small conference room across from your office. You make small talk for a few minutes, but it is clear that Taylor wants to get right down to business.

"Adrian, I have a pretty tight schedule today, so I think we should take 45 minutes to talk about the courageous-conversations framework here and then head to lunch. Does that sound okay? We should have enough time to talk through everything that I have learned about the fine art of having a candid conversation. My goal this afternoon is to help you learn how to create an environment where you can speak your mind without creating the impression that you are controlling the conversation, avoiding the issue, or competing for dominance. When done well, candid conversations provide the other party with the power to make a choice: The person can either accept and own the feedback and take steps towards improving the situation, or he or she can reject the feedback altogether, in which case you will need to make a decision, as this person's leader, about how you want to proceed next."

As Taylor speaks, you notice that he naturally demonstrates the courageous-conversation behaviors you talked about last week, and you make note of how he does it. He explicitly states the purpose of the conversation; he is unemotional but not cold; he clearly explains what he wants to accomplish and the time he has to do it; he describes your role in the exchange, both during this meeting and in future courageous conversations; he

is matter-of-fact but not arrogant in his tone. You know that this meeting is going to be very instructive.

Taylor pauses for a moment. Then he asks, "Are you okay with that?" You nod, thinking, *That's perfect. I like to get right to the heart of the matter.* Taylor motions towards the wall and asks whether he can use the whiteboard to list the key ingredients of a bold, direct, and courageous dialogue. You are grateful for this approach, saying, "That would be great, Taylor. I'm a visual learner, so seeing it in that format will work really well for me." Taylor grabs a set of colored markers, writes **Courageous Conversations Framework** on the board, and then turns to look at you.

"The first thing you need to know," Taylor says, "is that everyone wants to make courageous conversations complicated, but they're really not, so I'm going to keep it simple. However, sometimes simple is hard, especially for people who are really smart. Adrian, smart people like you want to elaborate on all kinds of topics, and all of a sudden, simple concepts become way too academic. The concepts underlying courageous conversations aren't abstract, and they aren't theoretical. The beauty of this framework is its simplicity."

Next, Taylor writes **Step #1: Prime the Conversation** on the whiteboard, saying, "I always have to remind myself of the importance of this step when I'm preparing to have a serious conversation with someone. Priming the conversation is the preparatory step, and the metaphor is straightforward: Before you can paint a wall, you have to roll a coat of primer on it. Otherwise, the paint won't set right, and you'll end up painting the whole wall a second time."

You remember putting some primer on the walls in your first apartment. The place was in pretty bad shape, and the pros at the home-improvement store told you that putting down a primer coat was a crucial first step. The full meaning of Taylor's message suddenly hits you, and you admit something embarrassing: "I don't think I ever primed Lee for the conversation. No wonder my message wasn't sticking. Instead of using a primer, I just rolled on a thicker coat of paint trying to make up for it, and that didn't work either."

Taylor smiles knowingly. "You've got the general idea. Primer is a preliminary step, and without it, your end product definitely suffers. I have a friend in the mining industry who thinks that the primer is like an electrical impulse that sets off an explosive charge. Another friend of mine works at a refinery, and for him, primer is a small pump that helps get an engine running. He uses the term 'prime the pump' all the time, and what he means is 'get it going.' My feeling is that no matter how you personally interpret the term, what you want is to have a controlled, intentional conversation, one where you've set the stage and begun with the right message using the right tone."

You nod your head thoughtfully, saying, "I get that. I understand that the general idea behind Step #1 is to notify the other person that this is not going to be a loose, casual conversation and to move the dialogue in a healthy, constructive direction from the outset."

Taylor nods. "This is where the shared control that we talked about earlier really begins. A good primer prepares the other party for what's coming and allows you to clearly and cleanly stake out your position. When you begin one of these deeper, richer conversations with Lee, you might

say something as simple as, 'Lee, I'm concerned about the apparent lack of progress you're making on your strategic plan, and I'd like to talk with you about it in depth and get your reaction to what I have to say.'"

"That's it?" you respond. "That's not too hard. You said it really simply, and I like how clear and assertive you were in the way you brought up the topic. If I were to say something like, 'Lee, I have some important thoughts and feedback that I want to share with you about your strategic plan. Can we talk about this now, or do you want to set up a time this afternoon?' would that work?"

"I think that would do the job, but if you approach it in that way, remember that you need to be really careful about asking questions. This is a time for making a statement. Tell her when you'd like to meet. If it doesn't work for her to meet right then, you can start the conversation again—with a primer, of course—in the afternoon."

"Okay." You are getting excited. "I'm getting the hang of this now. What's the next step? I can tell you've learned some other things about candid conversations that I've clearly been missing."

Taylor writes **Step #2: State Your Position** on the white board. "Stating your position is a critical step in this process. For those who tend to be minimizers, a healthy dose of real courage will be required here, because your position should clearly indicate what you perceive to be going on. It describes the issue, the concern, or the problem you see in the way that you see it. When stating your position, it's imperative that you're direct and to the point so that Lee doesn't have to guess what's really on your mind. You need to say exactly what you've been thinking. Priming the conversation tells Lee what you are there to discuss,

but stating your position forces you to verbally articulate your perception of the whole topic and to explore it more deeply than you would in a typical conversation.

"For example, you might say to Lee, 'I'm really concerned about the strategic-planning process. We have talked about your creating a complete draft of your strategic plan for Marketing, and you've repeatedly told me that you will produce one for me to review. I'm troubled because I haven't seen anything yet, and I feel like we may be missing some real opportunities to help Galaxy grow.' At that point, you've clearly stated your position, and you've said enough.

"Now Adrian, I have something to admit to you: I generally have to mentally rehearse the message I want to convey before I start talking. If I don't, sometimes I can be too evasive, and other times I can be too critical. In fact, I have been known to drift right into the attack mode and say things like, 'I have been waiting since the day you arrived for you to produce a strategic vision, and all I get are promises. You haven't produced a single thing yet, and it's driving me crazy!'"

You laugh a little uncomfortably, saying, "I can see the difference."

Taylor nods. "So, if I were to say something like, 'Hey Lee, if you aren't too busy, do you think you could possibly get me some ideas about the big strategic objective before the month is out?' what do you think Lee is going to take away from that?"

You think that's a really good point. "Well, if it were me," you answer, "I would probably put that request on the back burner at the bottom of my list of C-grade priorities."

"Exactly, Adrian. When you make a serious request, you have to use eye contact and body language indicating that you need to be taken seriously, but without you coming across as aggressive. All you need to do is lean forward, make eye contact, and state your expectations simply, firmly, and clearly: 'This is really important to me. I want to get going on this initiative, and I am not prepared to wait any longer.'"

"Taylor, I think I get it," you say. "It's about being assertive—being direct without being aggressive."

"It's as simple as that. At this point, you can step back and see where the conversation leads next. If you end up asking a bunch of leading questions or find that you needed to do more homework or come better prepared for the discussion, you were not ready to have a candid conversation. Do your due diligence. Gather the facts before you dive into a deep, heart-to-heart discussion. The purpose of stating your position isn't to do research: it's to draw attention to Lee's choices, priorities, and behaviors as you perceive them. Your perspective at this point is based on information that may be incomplete or flawed, which brings us to the third element of the framework." Taylor writes **Step #3: Explain Your Thinking** on the board.

You look at the words and furrow your brow. "What do you mean by 'Explain Your Thinking'? I thought you did that in Step 2."

"Not quite, Adrian. You've gone from priming the conversation to stating your position, but you haven't yet explained how you arrived at the conclusions you've drawn. The art of the courageous conversation is to take responsibility for your perspective and your position on the topic under discussion. You need to provide the rationale for your position in very clear terms. First, lay out the information you've gathered. You want to drill down to the very first layer of your thinking. Something has caught your attention. Maybe you've made an observation or collected information that has triggered some deliberation in your mind. Something has sparked your analysis; there is reason behind your current stance. What you want to reveal to Lee here is how you have interpreted that data. You want to demonstrate how you've come to your present perception or conclusion so she can follow your logic."

"How might that sound, Taylor? My biggest worry is that instead of moving the conversation forward in a healthy way, I'll revert to the behaviors I'm more comfortable with—avoiding or attacking. Sometimes my emotions and frustrations take over, I can feel myself heading down that path, and I have a hard time stopping myself from making those mistakes."

Taylor looks at you knowingly. "Adrian, I've seen you do that before. Your voice changes—it gains sort of a sharp edge—and I can tell that you are on the brink of exploding."

"Oh, wow. Is it that obvious?" you ask.

"Yes, it is. The pitch of your voice changes, as does the cadence of your speech. You sound really strained. Whenever this happens, I can tell that you are doing everything you can do to stay calm. Most of the time, you're just barely able to hold it together. Even when you manage to keep it contained, it's easy to see that the explosion has already gone off inside you.

"So here is a possibility. Tell me how this sounds to you: 'Lee, each week at our team meeting, I ask all team leaders to share the progress they are making with their strategic plans and how they intend to reinvent their teams in terms of the changes that Galaxy will face in the future. And at each meeting, I see you nod and smile, but when you talk about Marketing, you really only refer to the tactical fires that you're putting out. You talk a lot about crises and emergencies, as well as about your operational accomplishments, but I haven't heard you share your insights about the long-term intentions you have for your department.

'After seven months, I have come to the conclusion that developing a strategic plan really isn't a serious priority for you. Other managers in the business are looking to Marketing for some insight into how you plan to move forward, because that is an area that your predecessor never addressed. And because you've now been in the position for seven months and nothing has changed in that area, a lot of people are starting to get really worried that we are losing valuable time."'

"Can you see it, Adrian? You've said just enough. You have about a minute, give or take, to lay out the topography of your thinking. Where did your position come from? How did it evolve? What impact is the behavior having? What kinds of evidence do you have? I think if you can be open and use this opportunity to show Lee how you reached your position, you've done your job. We minimizers have to step up. You'll need to let go of what's comfortable and easy in order to be clear and direct with Lee. This will put Lee under the microscope, and it's going to be a little uncomfortable for her—and for you.

"Now, you need to know that Lee may intentionally or unintentionally become defensive as you explain your thinking. She might interrupt you. She could try to blame others, deflect, defer, or point fingers. This is something you'll really need to watch out for. If you take the bait and become overly aggressive while discussing Lee's obstacles and excuses, the conversation can quickly turn from a rational discussion into a mud-slinging, negativity-creating, contentious, truly nasty debate. If that happens, it's almost inevitable that your mindset will shift, and you'll begin viewing this conversation as a competition. You'll throw all the evidence you have directly at Lee, doing everything in your power to prove why you're right and she's not. People who have win/compete tendencies are highly skilled in this way. Like good trial attorneys, they know just how to win debates. But given the gravity of the situation you're in with Lee, you can't let yourself be swept away. You have to keep a level head, even when the conversation gets tense. And if you can, you should do your best to get to Step #4 before Lee has a chance to interrupt you."

You are eager for Taylor to provide more insight and watch carefully as he writes, **Step #4: Test Their Understanding**.

"What do you mean by 'Test Their Understanding'?" you ask.

"At this moment in the courageous conversation, you have to find out where Lee stands, and as hard as it may be, you need to try to keep the conversation focused on the issue. It's easy to veer off track and focus on your own feelings, other people who may be to blame, obstacles and distractions getting in Lee's way, and so on. When you test her thinking, you'll do so by asking Lee a few simple questions, such as 'Lee, what do you think about this?

Is the data I've gathered accurate? Does my logic make sense? What am I missing?' Keep it short and sweet. You have two goals here: Draw Lee's attention to the facts you have before you, and then draw her attention to the conclusions you have made in relation to those facts. This technique invites the other person into the conversation in a responsible way.

"However, I'll caution you that Lee may still view this as an invitation to vent her frustrations or blame other people, especially if she sees things in a way that differs from your own. Now, the winner/competitor in you doesn't want the other person to see things differently because you are so attached to your perspective and the belief that you can't possibly be wrong. Because of this, testing her understanding will require you to be a little bit vulnerable. When you candidly explain how you arrived at your position—as objectively and reasonably as you can—you are exposing your rationale and your personal perspective. If you are a minimizer, Step #4 could be really uncomfortable for you. You may bring some painful issues to light; you might discover that, in all likelihood, you have contributed to the problem.

"Adrian, I think the message in all of this is that you simply cannot have any hidden agendas. You have to be genuine when you communicate. You need to convey that you are truly interested in hearing her reactions and understanding her emotions, regardless of whether what she says is entirely correct or appropriate. Collaboration begins when you let people know that you are genuinely interested in hearing what they have to say and fully understanding the situation.

"This process is very similar to the scientific method. Think of Step 3 as a hypothesis. In order to be validated or invalidated, your hypothesis must be tested. Step #4 is designed to give you that opportunity. You have gathered the information, have come to some sound conclusions about what you think is happening, and are now trying to test your logic. Your aim is to gather valid information so you can interpret the situation correctly, make informed choices, and create an environment conducive to gaining everyone's personal commitment. Everybody has to want to ferret out and resolve the real issues. Testing their understanding is a very powerful way to start moving towards that goal. It will demonstrate your desire to be open, receptive, and respectful of their viewpoints and should help lessen any tension present in the conversation. This should decrease any need your team members have to compete against you, win the argument, defend undesirable behavior, or deflect personal responsibility. You aren't conceding your viewpoint at this stage; you are simply looking for a reaction, trying to discover any data you may not already have, and inviting the other parties to participate fully in the conversation."

"Is that all there is to it, Taylor?" you ask.

"Almost. The final step in getting these courageous conversations off to a good start is **Step #5: Explore Their Thinking**." He writes it down. "You do this through inquiry."

"Inquiry? What do you mean?"

Taylor answers, "Well, in this context *inquiry* means that you have to probe a bit. Make an effort to discover how she understands the reality of the situation. Where is she coming from? What data does she have access to that

you may not? In what ways is she interpreting the same data differently from you? Are the conclusions that she is drawing incorrect? Is she making assumptions? Is she misinterpreting anything?

Through inquiry, exploration, and working hard to understand the other person's perspective, you will begin to see where the disagreement resides and why these differences in perspective exist. You can use this as a teaching moment, an opportunity to broaden her perspective or your own, or to talk about something that went unnoticed before. Each of you should come away from the conversation with a fresh pair of eyes. Your mutually broadened perspective will help improve your relationship with the person, as well as your ability to assess and analyze the situation under discussion much more accurately.

"I'll give you a couple of quick tips, Adrian. When you feel the 'winning' tendency start to creep in, do a little more testing and inquiry. When you feel the conversation is going nowhere, emphasize your position more strongly and do some additional thinking. When you use these two tips in tandem, you'll bring both rigor and balance to difficult dialogue that has the potential to be highly emotionally charged."

Taylor steps back from the whiteboard and you can see the whole process. "Adrian, this process isn't a cure-all, but it is an effective and usable technique that I've used time and again to cut to the core of an issue. Once you master this process, all of the other skills you have—developing a plan of action, having follow-up conversations, coaching for performance improvement and professional development—can be used to much better effect. And don't forget that once Lee starts to make improvements, you can use

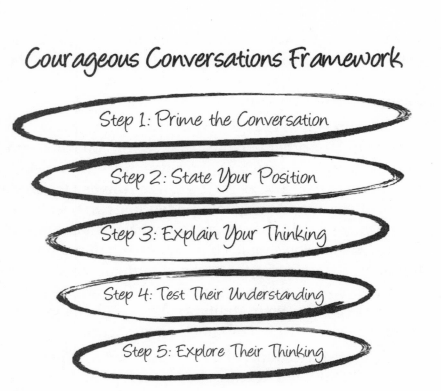

Courageous Conversations Framework

Step 1: Prime the Conversation

Step 2: State Your Position

Step 3: Explain Your Thinking

Step 4: Test Their Understanding

Step 5: Explore Their Thinking

this same technique to give her positive feedback and encouragement."

"That's a great idea," you say. "Quite frankly, I think I could even benefit from using this technique in my own weekly team meetings. I sometimes feel like I'm talking around the issues during those meetings, and it bothers me when everyone is looking at everyone else like, 'It's not my problem.' I'm sure this framework would help me bring a lot more out into the open in those meetings."

Taylor smiles broadly, "That's right, Adrian. It's a tool that can work in many settings. Whenever I feel especially passionate about something, or feel that something important is being overlooked, this is the approach I use. It helps me work more effectively with other people so that we don't miss any opportunities. Honestly, Adrian, I use this simple five-step framework everywhere I go. I just wish I had started using it sooner—in my life and in my career. If you choose to use it, I hope it works as well for you as it has for me."

You are so grateful that Taylor is sharing his time and technique with you, and you can hardly get the words out fast enough, saying, "Taylor, this has been so helpful to me. I promised I'd only take 45 minutes of your time, and here we are. Over an hour's gone by, and I really, really appreciate everything you've done. Now that I look back on it, I actually think that Lee used a similar approach with me the other day. She did a bang-up job with it, by the way."

Taylor smiles, saying, "I'll take your word for it. So, do you think you want to try this out?"

You smile sheepishly. "Even if I didn't like this framework, which I do, I wouldn't have a choice but to use it. Especially right now. It's time to do or die. One way or another, I have to have a meeting of the minds with Lee. One way or another I will help this organization move forward. Now is the time. And I still believe that Lee is the person to help us do it.

"But right now, I think she's stuck. She's gotten into the habit of doing what many of us would do: responding to the crisis of the moment. And, frankly, she's really good at resolving this week's disasters. I just need to help her learn how to anticipate future issues so she can use that talent in a longer-term capacity. I think that if we can broach these sticky issues by having a courageous conversation, we can pool our intellect and figure out a way to get over this hump.

"We've got to get to the bottom of this, and we need to be able to make informed choices about whether she can move forward, whether she wants to move forward, whether she needs some help with her strategy, and whether she can offer innovative ideas to the Marketing department and Galaxy as a whole from this point forward. Taylor, I think that if we can get everything out in the open, figuring out where to go, what to do, what kinds of resources we'll need, and when to begin should be a whole lot easier."

Taylor agrees with you completely. "You know where you need to go next. Let me know how it goes and if I can help. You know where to reach me."

"I owe you a lot, Taylor," you say excitedly as you walk together out to the parking lot. "Thanks so much for all your help. Now, let's go get some lunch!"

EIGHT

Preparing for the Team Meeting

Y ou are on the train again, heading home, and as a result of your meeting with Taylor, a lot of thoughts are going through your mind. It has become abundantly clear to you that orchestrating a bold, open, courageous discussion is not about changing others as much as it is about identifying and being aware of your own ineffective patterns of communicating and candidly explaining your point of view to the people around you.

You are feeling encouraged by the simplicity of the framework that Taylor shared with you. It is nothing more than a robust skill set that requires presence of mind, a focused message, and some ongoing practice. It occurs to you that learning to facilitate a courageous conversation is just like learning to play a musical instrument, or mas-

tering a foreign language. Mastery requires commitment and a willingness to practice and apply the skills.

You know that you have to do this really soon. If you don't, you will lose all the momentum that you have gained from the ups and downs with Lee and the instruction that Taylor has given you. You search your mind for the ideal practice scenario, one that will be perfect for the task. None of the situations seem ideal, but you quickly realize that is the whole point: No situation is textbook perfect. You can apply these five essential skills to virtually any situation.

You ask yourself what you have on the docket tomorrow, and it hits you: Your mid-week team meeting, scheduled for tomorrow morning, will give you an excellent opportunity to try out the skills. You lead a small team of only four direct reports, Lee and three others. You begin thinking a little about your team and the things it hasn't managed to accomplish in the last year. The more you think about it, the more it occurs to you that the rest of the team is in the same boat as Lee. Everyone has been dodging the strategic imperative that you thought had been well communicated. Everyone seems apprehensive about taking solid action and charting a path forward. They are all sitting around waiting for senior leadership to provide a perfect path. For the most part, they merely want to ride along, believing that strategy is someone else's work, something that people who are higher up in the organization need to worry about. Most importantly, you realize that you haven't taken accountability for strategic results very seriously and that you've minimized your expectations of team members. You can tell that this is an opportunity for your team to help the entire organization

understand strategy as something that everyone should think about (and contribute to), not something that is strictly relegated to the realm of senior leadership.

This next team meeting is a perfect opportunity to practice the courageous-conversations concepts with your own group in preparation for changing the way strategic imperatives (and other important information) will be communicated across the entire organization in the future. In your mind's eye, you see this as no different from any other frank, candid, one-on-one conversation. It occurs to you that one of the most important actions you need to take before initiating this team conversation is some simple preparation.

Taylor referred to that during one of your early conversations, saying, "There are three things to keep in mind before you make a decision to begin a candid conversation and dive deeply into an important piece of business. Number one: Ask yourself why this conversation needs to happen. Number two: Examine your motive and intent. Number three: Ask yourself what you hope to gain and what outcomes you want to achieve by engaging in this dialogue."

The first question is pretty easy for you to answer, as you have already done a little bit of preparation. You feel as though it's right in line with your perception that no one is stepping up and taking responsibility for helping Galaxy position itself to take on big opportunities. You think that strategy really needs to come from both the "top down" and the "bottom up," and that all four of your team leaders could play a significant role in this process. You believe that your team can demonstrate how to look at the signs on the horizon and make preparations that will help

shape the future of the business. The initial preparation component of the conversation is easy.

The more difficult question to answer is that of your motives. What are your true intentions? At first, you had wanted to use this meeting to chide, ridicule, and punish your team members for letting you down. But as you think about it more clearly, you realize the downsides of this approach and decide that you'd rather give your group the opportunity to shine, to lead the way for the rest of the organization. Your next thought is that this will be a good opportunity for you and your direct reports. But as you think about it more deeply, you come to the conclusion that all of these motivations are pretty shallow and self-serving. You realize that what this whole exercise is really designed to do is to ensure that your team remains relevant and continues to add value to the business. By being more proactive, your team can help the business build its long-term competitive advantage. If only you can help your team capture the vision that their actions and abilities to change the "business-as-usual" mentality will help Galaxy achieve the differentiation it needs in a crowded marketplace.

You realize that, at the moment, no one is rocking the boat. No one is challenging the status quo. No one is taking risks or making big bets—or even making little bets, for that matter. The whole organization is currently operating from a "wait-and-see" perspective, and that simply won't work long term. Everyone claims that they are buried with the day-to-day routine. They are caught in the tactical-activity trap. You believe in your heart that this focus has to change. At some point, more people have to be willing to admit that short-term thinking is not the path to long-term success—and they'll have to say so out loud. If you can begin to break the cycle of tactically motivated action, starting with your own group, they can serve as a powerful example to everyone in the organization about how important it is to discover and employ a unique strategic-contribution concept.

Defining the true purpose of the courageous conversation you are planning to have with your team feels really good! This conversation is not about looking good or winning for the sake of winning: it is about the survival of the business. Its true goal is to ensure that the business remains stable and profitable, thereby protecting the livelihoods of a lot of people.

The third aspect of the preparation phase that Taylor emphasized is the outcome. What are you hoping to get out of this interaction? What is the takeaway? This one is a little harder to pin down. In some ways, you would like your team to go boldly forward, to take giant steps. But as the train carries you home, something else hits you. Over the years, Taylor has often told you, "Sometimes, simple is hard."

You have always known that the first step is often the hardest one to take, so you ask yourself, "What is the simplest first step forward? What is the takeaway or outcome that will ignite some momentum?" You try to think of something that will be simple to manage while you are simultaneously trying to transform your own team and the way it thinks. After some thought, you finally settle on one idea: The outcome that you are looking for is a collection of strategic ideas, not an elaborate strategic plan. All you want is a list of three or four strategic moves being

considered by each of your managers. That is the request, and that is the outcome you desire.

If you can create some alignment between the strategic initiatives offered by each of your managers, your whole team will take a huge step forward, enabling the organization's managers to start looking at the business' future rather than its past. For now, having each manager identify just a few critical changes that will make a long-term difference in the way your function operates will be an enormous breakthrough.

You realize that reflecting on those three questions hasn't been so hard, and having the answers in front of you will make a huge difference in the conversation to come. The answers to those three little questions—"Why have the conversation?" "What is your motive?" and "What do you hope to get out of it?"—should lead you successfully forward. It seems so simple.

But you are a realist. You know that no conversation ever goes exactly as planned. You'll need to be prepared to respond on the fly; you'll have to be ready for the unexpected. But at the same time, you also need to run the conversation through your mind, envisioning how all of this might play out, just as a way to get things rolling. You decide to frame the issue using the techniques that Taylor shared with you, listening to yourself and articulating it in the way he has shown you. You lay a script out in your mind:

Priming the conversation and explaining your position will be really simple. All you need to say is something like, "I have a concern that I would like to share with all of you. I want to begin by explaining my thinking about it, and then I want to get your reactions. Earlier this year,

I thought we had all agreed to create a strategic direction for each of our areas of responsibility. We are now eight months into the year, and I haven't seen any of them yet."

As you think about the way you want to articulate your position, you decide that you want to keep it very simple and very succinct, to remain unemotional, to remove any edge from your voice. You want to share the circumstances as you see them in a matter-of-fact tone. Years ago, one of your leadership program facilitators had said it this way: "Let the words confront and the tone support." Knowing your team, you acknowledge that you are going to get a little pushback, a little resistance. People are going to say, "Well, we talked about it," or "I didn't think we had agreed to it," or "We didn't set a date for when they had to be turned in," or "We have been incredibly busy with product rollouts and customer issues," and so on.

You know that you will have to be prepared for some of these excuses, valid or not, because some level of resistance and defensiveness is natural when people feel the weight of accountability land squarely on their shoulders. You will have to be careful to avoid taking any bait that would allow this conversation to turn into an argument or gripe session. It won't be productive to focus too heavily on their objections or excuses. The best response will be for you to acknowledge how challenging it is to balance the tactical and operational demands of the job with the strategic elements.

Once you've given voice to their concerns, you can simply emphasize your desire to have an open discussion about the realities of this issue. You'll need to reaffirm your intent: Your team members need to know that inflicting pain or being unreasonable is not your goal. You can simply say, "I realize that this is a dilemma and together, we should be able to figure out a way forward." It's important to remember that this may not resolve any of their frustration, irritation, or anxiety about moving into a more forward-looking and proactive frame of mind, but it is a step in the right direction nonetheless. The key here is simply to listen, be patient, and explain the rationale for your assertions.

As you think through the conversation you want to have, you feel the best way to begin the third step in Taylor's process will be to simply say, "I believe all of us understand intellectually that being more proactive and more strategic makes a lot of sense. I believe that our parts of the business—those of us in business development, marketing, and advertising—are really the 'point of the spear' when it comes to helping Galaxy move to the next level. I also think that we could be waiting a long, long time if we believe that we need a perfect path or a detailed plan from the top to get us moving. I just don't know if that will ever happen in the way we hope. Many signals are coming from the senior leadership team that should give us ideas on how we need to transform our function or move our piece of the value chain of activities forward. Using senior management as a barrier to developing a vision or plan for how each of us can unlock more value and help the business compete against our rivals simply isn't helpful."

You know that some people on your team will react with cynicism. You can almost hear them saying, "That's all well and good, but the real issue is how we're supposed to find the time and the resources we need to do things differently while still being operationally efficient." You realize that you'll probably have to offer the team some additional insight before you test their understanding and ask for their response. This is a moment where you'll need to say something like, "Let me explain my view of this resource issue and how I've reconciled it in my mind. Once I've explained my take on the situation, I'd like to hear what you are thinking.

All of us spend time on certain activities that don't really benefit us. It's easy to get caught up in unproductive tasks. We all do it. I think that if we put our minds to it, we can easily find under-utilized resources, people, and time to devote to our strategic obligations. I also believe that much of the strategic work that needs to be done is not about time management: it's about mind management. It's more about the discipline of thinking through our options, making the right choices, and prioritizing our tasks. And much of that activity isn't actually a time or scheduling issue. We just need to focus our attention on strategic thinking about innovative ways of producing our services and products. What do you think?"

At this stage of the conversation, you need to test your logic with the team by asking them for their thoughts. Your question can be something as simple as, "Do you see it differently?" or "What is your take?" or "What is your perspective on delivering results today while still having enough energy and focus to help shape the future?" This is a good way to invite all of your team members into the conversation. The person inside you who wants to "win" and "sell" will try to push your perspective really hard and close the deal because you believe that you are right. You also know that this "testing" phase will make you vulnerable. You will be exposing your logic and rationale

to further scrutiny; there's even the possibility that you'll stand corrected by your team. You hate to be proven wrong. You have to be very genuine if you are going to encourage them to help frame an accurate perspective of the challenge you face.

At this point, you can begin to finish up with the last piece of the candid-conversations puzzle: inquiry. Inquire about their point of view and about the possibilities. Listening to their take on the situation will be a great opportunity for learning and discovery. This is a time for you to ask questions, test their logic, and construct a point of view with which everyone can take ownership. You also make a mental note to remind yourself to thank the group for their position, for their thoughtful and rational dialogue, and for giving you an opportunity to test their ideas.

Before you close the meeting, you'll need to ask the group for next steps. Tell them that you'd like them to devise a simple, doable plan of action. Be sensitive towards your team members, and acknowledge any team-member apprehension by saying, "All change has a price. It is going to create some discomfort. But the benefits of the change are larger than the cost or the pain of making a change." If they can see an opportunity to make a fundamental difference in the way the business is run by taking a few small steps forward, any resistance you encounter will be more manageable, and ultimately, it will dissipate.

As the train approaches your station, you realize that this candid conversation has the potential to be short and sweet, or substantially longer—depending on how everything goes. But if this issue is important, if this is a high-stakes topic, the time it takes to have the conversation will be worth every second. Accountability isn't free. Keeping a group focused on the important stuff takes investment. It also takes time—as well as courage and a willingness to be open to new ideas and points of view. You cannot be too certain, too set in your ways. You must anticipate the unexpected and, when appropriate, be open to its wisdom. If you want a culture of accountability and candor in your team, you have to show its members how to tackle complex, sensitive issues clearly and rationally.

You truly believe that this is something that is missing in your team and, to some degree, throughout the whole organization. Everyone needs to learn how to have courageous conversations, to be honest, forthright, and a good listener. You can't go ballistic. You will need to develop some patience, and as you do, things will come into focus. With these skills in hand, all kinds of difficult conversations may become just a little bit easier.

NINE

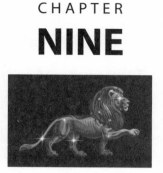

The Next Conversation

D uring your early-morning workout on the treadmill, the upcoming meeting with your team weighs heavily on your mind. Even as you watch the early-morning business program on TV, you find yourself trying to envision how the whole meeting will play out. One moment, your thoughts drift to a "minimize" stance. You think to yourself, *Why not forget this whole thing?* The rest of the organization is pretty happy with everyone on your team except Lee. So why risk ruffling the feathers of your team members? Why urge the team on and hold them accountable for being more innovative—for being proactive shapers of the future? You even experience real doubts about your own ability to put together a strategy.

In the next moment, your mind vacillates and the pendulum swings to the other side. You feel anger, frustration, and disappointment. Why haven't these so-called "managers" been able to fulfill your requests from earlier in the year? Maybe it would be appropriate to be a little more combative, a little more punitive, a little more aggressive. Why can't leaders at this level just follow instructions? They are good business people; why don't they use their brains? Why can't they see the need to make Galaxy more competitive? Are they so wrapped up in day-to-day operations that they don't recognize the benefits of being more forward-looking?

But later on, as you ride the train to work, you make a firm commitment to do what Taylor recommended: Just trust the process. You have a game plan outlined for this conversation. You are hoping that in the time you have available, you'll be able to get to the heart of the issue. As you have a candid conversation with yourself prior to the meeting, you begin to feel a renewed sense of confidence. You feel sure you can land this conversation right in the sweet spot. In fact, you begin to eagerly look forward to the opportunity to practice your courageous-conversations skills with your team this morning, because you know you need more practice if this is going to become your standard operating procedure. And an hour and thirty minutes later, after the meeting ends, your cell phone rings. To your pleasant surprise, Taylor is right there. He has always been a good ally, and he never forgets.

You are on your way to lunch when the call comes in. Taylor, in his usual style, asks, "Do you have time to give me an update?"

Your reaction is very simple, "Sure. Actually, there isn't a lot to say. The meeting went as well as I could have expected. It took me less than ten minutes to prime the conversation and set the stage, state my position, and explain my logic. Then, I invited the team to test and clarify my theory. I opened the meeting up for twenty minutes of inquiry and where to go next."

You tell Taylor that you had anticipated that the conversation might deteriorate into a long argument, maybe even an hour-long debate with lots of finger pointing and placing of blame. Taylor acknowledges that sometimes that happens when you have been in a culture where people are not used to discussing the "un-discussable." When people begin to open up and talk about what they really see and how they really feel, it can be quite a shock.

Taylor asks you if there were any big surprises, any breakthroughs in the whole interaction. You say, "The only breakthrough I had was how quickly the team learns. In fact, before this meeting ended, one of the team members spoke up and courageously shared something of their own."

Taylor asks, "Can I guess who that is?"

You say, "Sure. It probably won't be a shock to you."

Taylor's guess was spot on: "Lee." You respond affirmatively. Then Taylor asks, "What was the message?"

You say, "Well, Lee boldly spoke out about the real elephant in the room. She said, 'Judging both from your reaction and the team's, we are all pushing on this open door, this expectation of being more strategic, and I have two thoughts: Number one is no one has ever shown us, and we have never been taught in any of our past training, how to create strategy in the middle of the organization, how to create strategy for the critical activity or function inside the business. We have been taught strategy from the classic Harvard, Wharton, or Stanford corporate competitive-strategy models.' She courageously suggested—not demanded—suggested that this team needs a bit of training on how to transfer and adopt business strategy for their functions—not just how to do a long-range plan based on our current operating model, but something designed to be bold and exciting, something that would help us reinvent our functions, find redundancies, and introduce new services and products to our own internal customers as well external customers.

"I have to admit I was a little shocked that Lee was ahead of me on this one. I decided to just let her talk. She didn't take much longer, just said, 'There are a few resources out there.' But I was even more shocked when she said, 'Adrian has been pushing me pretty hard to take some risks and scope out a strategy. So for the last few days, when I have been able to find some time, I have searched the Internet and done some research, even checked out a couple of good books on how people like us build a game-changing strategy from the inside. When we get out of this meeting, I will send you a few links that might be helpful for all of us.

'But that's not the most important thing I want to share. My second thought is that it would be most helpful if we all had an overarching strategy from you, Adrian—something that we can map to, something that we can align ourselves around, a strategy that can band us all together. I think we're better together. We come to these meetings, and we share information. We all talk about what's going on in our own little silos within our team. We're all respectful, we all provide information, but we don't have a task or strategy to perform that we own jointly. I think we are a great group of individuals; we are a good work group. I just think we are missing the boat when it comes to working as a real team, and I think this is an opportunity where we can all work collaboratively, own this strategy thing, and be accountable to each other, not just to you, Adrian. We all have responsibility to create, execute, and be accountable to each other collectively."

"Wow, Taylor, I have to tell you; this was a shocker. I thought, first of all, that I was going to get the most push-back from Lee after I had fumbled the ball with her for the past several months. I wasn't expecting that she would be out there leading the charge. Secondly, she effectively called me out because I haven't been walking the talk. She's right; I haven't offered up anything in terms of my vision. If I were able to cascade down even an outline of my vision of the future, and if I were to share my view of the variables and what I am sensing from senior leadership, this team would have a much easier time thinking and acting more proactively. Furthermore, I think Lee is right: This is work that we should all own collectively."

"So," Taylor asks, "what's the next big move?"

"Well, we all agreed that starting in two weeks, we will begin a series of three half-day strategic retreats of our own. We will all have work to do each week prior to our mini offsite retreat. And within a month, our goal will be to roll our strategy up to the senior team for a little critique. We'll encourage them to give us some feedback on our ideas. Everyone on the team is pretty enthusiastic about this approach."

Taylor says encouragingly, "I can tell you are excited, and I am looking forward to hearing about how things unfold as you and your team get more accustomed to having candid conversations, I'd love to hear how it goes if you have the time. And if not, it's totally okay. I know you've got a lot to do. You have a big agenda ahead of you. "

You joke a little bit and say, "I might have to put you on retainer!"

With his customary good humor, Taylor answers, "My only retainer is a good sushi lunch." With that, Taylor ends his call, saying, "You always know how to reach me. If I can be of some help, I'm always there for you to talk to. And Adrian, the only thing I ask of you is that you spread the wealth. If this is a method that works for you, share it with others and don't give up. It's not going to be perfect every time. There will be those moments when people don't respond the way you want or wish they would. And that's why it's not a technique; it's really not even a tool. It's just a process, and words matter in the process. It's a way of being, and I think you've gotten the hang of it. I hope we get to talk again soon."

TEN

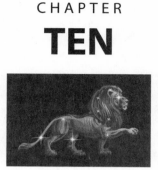

One More Courageous Conversation

You sit across the table from Taylor at your regular sushi restaurant. It has been about a year since you held your first candid conversation with your team, and you are grateful for your friendship with Taylor. The two of you have been meeting for lunch at least once a month. You truly value the insights Taylor provides and the fact that he often prompts you to engage in self-reflection. The lunches have also been a good way for you to follow through with actually using the process because you know Taylor will ask about how it's going. You order your "usual" and regale Taylor with highlights from your recent vacation and the latest on your family. Taylor listens as he sips his tea, but, as expected, he interjects, "So, tell me about the next big conversation you need or want to have."

"Well, Taylor, that one is a little tricky."

Taylor responds with a chuckle in his voice. "Am I hearing some minimizing going on?"

"Yeah, you probably are."

"Why?" Taylor asks.

"Well, this one is a little tricky because it's with Kerry, the Chief Operating Officer."

"Why does that seem tricky?"

"What's been happening with me is really happening with the senior team."

"How so?"

"Well, I don't believe that the senior team has to create this big, formal strategic document, but I do believe that our senior team could and should sponsor more strategic conversations, more strategic communication and idea sharing, maybe even some forums or round-table discussions so people can get together and share innovative ideas about how to approach the future. Galaxy has definitely had some recent success, but I think people need to know what's next, what the strategy is now. Shouldn't senior management give them a better strategic framework? Besides, they wanted Lee to do it; so shouldn't everyone?"

"Why don't you just talk to the COO, explain your position, and share your logic and rationale? Give him a chance to test your thinking. And also give him a chance to come up with his own thoughts on this concept?"

"Well, Taylor, I am afraid that Kerry is going to be a little embarrassed by this whole thing and by not having something in place already. I don't want to be too presumptuous. I don't even know if it is my right to coach up."

Taylor interrupts abruptly, saying, "Adrian, it is your right to coach up in your role. You are a vice president. No senior executive can see all of the landscape. You've got to be bold. You can't just play it safe and hope that somehow people will magically have an epiphany, that they'll somehow discover what you are doing and what you are seeing and the needs and problems that are out there. That's why businesses have good people like you. They want the opportunity to discuss the sensitive, 'undiscussable' issues that you described. Adrian, businesses fail because people like you, who could choose to do a few things differently, fail to speak up. Staying quiet won't help Galaxy prosper. You've got to make some noise." Then he tests you, "What's wrong with the way I'm seeing this, Adrian? What am I missing?"

You can see it: you can see Taylor right there, right then, using the process with you. Not long afterwards, he asks, "So what do you think you can do? How can you broach that conversation?" You respond with a smile, "Let me do a little preparation. You know from the events of the past how important preparation is."

You return from lunch thinking about Taylor's advice. You barely sit down at your desk when the COO, Kerry, barges into your office unannounced and flatly states, "How did you do it?" You never would have guessed that the opportunity for this conversation would come up so quickly.

"How did I do what?"

He asks excitedly, "You mean, you didn't see the profile on Galaxy in the trade publications last Friday? How exactly did you turn Lee and the Marketing team around?"

You have to confess that while you were on vacation last week, you missed all the fuss in the media about Galaxy.

Kerry continues, "The author had glowing praise for the remarkable work that is being done in both Marketing and Galaxy's IT function that is saving us a bundle with the innovative shared-services strategy.

You ask, "So what did they say about Marketing specifically?"

"It's all right here." Kerry gives you a copy of the story. You start skimming the article that the author wrote on the basis of a series of interviews with you and many other executives last month.

The first line really grabs your attention: "After being a perennial under-performer in the market, Galaxy is finally on the radar screen and sending notice to all the big pharma players that they no longer control the marketplace." The article goes on to say that Galaxy is building a reputation of reliability with its customers and delivering superior financial returns to its shareholders: "Thanks in part to a progressive Marketing department, Galaxy is now all the rage in social media, and aggressive search-engine marketing efforts have increased market presence and customer awareness. Healthcare professionals have discovered the powerful solutions that Galaxy is providing for specific disease indications. The Marketing department has participated in, or is directly sponsoring, all kinds of relevant events and shows, which is adding to Galaxy's recent success."

You read on: "Galaxy has now opened affiliate offices in five major Pacific Rim cities and plans to hire a permanent, full-time staff in Hong Kong very soon. Sales are trending up, new products are coming down the research pipeline, and clinical trials are going well. What's not to like about Galaxy's success? Market analysts even estimate that Galaxy stock will trade at least 25 percent above its current fair market value before the end of the year." You look up with a smile.

"Wow!" Kerry exclaims. "Adrian, do you know what this means for our careers and stock options? If we continue down this path, we could hit the jackpot."

"Yeah! This is stunning news," you agree.

"So Adrian, I need to know how you pulled this off. I know IT gets some credit for this too, but how did you actually ignite this change in the Marketing department?"

Over the past 12 months, you have given that question a lot of thought, so it is easy for you to respond. "Kerry, there are a lot of reasons why Marketing is in much better shape. First and foremost, I think we finally have the 'right people in the right seats on the bus,' as Jim Collins said in *Good to Great*. But more importantly, we have the right type of bus going in the right direction. I don't exactly know the formula that the IT group is using, but I can tell you what has worked for us.

"Honestly speaking, our story is simply built on a culture of communication that is open, transparent, and bold; it has allowed us to get Marketing on the right track. Everyone in my organization has adopted a set of communication principles and beliefs that were laid out to me a little over a year ago by a trusted mentor. And the approach came with a promise that if we would rigorously follow these beliefs and processes, we would be able to have valuable conversations about how to put the Marketing part of the organization in a better position, help the business be more strategic, and capture new business opportunities."

You hand Kerry a small, laminated card that sits on your desk: "Kerry, it is all right here. I keep this diagram of the communication process I structured that day with the help of my long-time business friend and mentor, Taylor Vanderpool. Without these principles, we would still be dancing around some of our most difficult decisions, challenges, and issues. Without these five simple skills, I'm convinced I would be vacillating between avoiding emotionally charged issues on one hand or going into attack mode to win and dominate every debate on the other hand—not to mention that Lee might not have made it here at Galaxy."

Kerry seems intrigued, so you continue: "The old way was not a good formula for us. People were simply not telling me what they thought, sharing feedback with each other, giving direction, or holding others accountable. And when people did speak up and put their cards on the table, others got defensive. I discovered that this was a problem that went far beyond Lee and her Marketing department. Call it dumb luck, circumstance, or timing; it just happened that Lee and her team were in the crosshairs and getting scrutinized for a variety of reasons when she joined the organization. We made zero strategic progress until we were able to sit down and candidly address the most pressing issues that were preventing us from going to the next level of performance.

"I have to be honest with you, Kerry. For the first several months after Lee and I finally got on the same page, the progress was still uneven and bumpy. It took Lee and her team several weeks just to cobble together an innovative, strategic agenda to take the Marketing department to the next level and help us grow the business. This wasn't easy on Lee. She encountered a lot of pushback from some of her people. But she was smart. She started to use these same five principles to have her own courageous coaching conversations. She shared feedback honestly and boldly confronted the issues and conflicts within her team.

"You may not be aware of this, but she discovered that two of her people were simply doing just enough to get by, trying really hard not to get caught performing poorly. They were not fit for the rigorous transformation that she needed to accomplish. We ultimately came to the conclusion that if people on her team didn't have the sea legs for an exciting, strategic voyage, it would be better to respectfully help them move off the team and into a different role. Lee also started to have a lot of upward courageous conversations with me.

"The majority of her crew seemed to catch fire. Today, they are definitely engaged and energized by the opportunity to help shape the destiny of their team and the business. It has required a lot of commitment and hard work balancing the demands of the day-to-day tasks while investing energy, time, and resources in the future success of the business. Lee told me just a few weeks ago that she is committed to making all of her conversations more open, rich, and deep with her team members. Not every conversation Lee has needs to be intense. But what she has done is become very clear in all of her communications so people understand her expectations and where she stands. When it is time for her to give people honest direction, there is no gamesmanship or guesswork, and

she definitely doesn't ask forty questions like you see in some communication models.

"I have read a few books on this topic, and it seems that many popular communication and coaching models are built around cleverly disguised manipulation: leading the other person to your point of view using clever questions. I believe the key to business success here at Galaxy is holding more honest, heartfelt discussions about the challenges that come up every day in every department, especially when you are trying to grow a business and make a real impact on the marketplace." Kerry nods in agreement and seems fascinated.

You continue, "Look Kerry, I hope you won't think I am out of line, and I hope that what I am about to share with you won't create any ill will between us. I think more open, transparent, clear communication needs to flow downward, as well as upward, through the organization."

"Okay. I agree with that."

"So if you will permit me, let me try the process with you. I would be curious to see how you respond to it."

Kerry looks a little shocked for a moment and then cautiously agrees to let you try. "All right; go for it. I am curious about the feedback you have for me."

You decide that this is the moment to apply the skills and speak your mind. So you dive in and say, in a very matter-of-fact tone, "Kerry, I am concerned about the lack of progress I see in many departments when it comes to their strategic agendas and initiatives. You play an important role in making that happen. At Galaxy, too many people are simply working *in* the business and not working *on* the business. If you are willing to listen, I would like

to explain what I see happening with your colleagues in senior management."

You pause and think, *Wow! That came out pretty well.*

It takes Kerry a few seconds before he responds. Half-jokingly he says, "Is this something you are going to beat me up over?"

You smile and say, "I stopped the beatings in my division 12 months ago."

Kerry seems to acknowledge your point and says, "Go on. I am all ears. I am a big believer in constructive criticism."

You think, *Okay, this is the perfect time to state my position. This will be pretty easy because I have been ruminating on this for a long time.* You have asked yourself many times why the other divisions and functions were not pulling their weight on a more strategic level, especially after people were so anxious for Lee to do it over 12 months ago.

You courageously proceed. "I am worried about many of the other functions in the company and their lack of forward-looking, long-term planning to take their functions to the next level. Many of the other departments have been curious about the changes going on in the Marketing department, and I have carefully shared some of the strategies we have been working on, including the communication process. But so far, no one seems to be making any progress; and the executive team, quite candidly, has yet to share a strategic vision, or a strategic agenda, or any key initiatives that would help departments and teams create strategies that reflect that vision. So Kerry, I have come to the conclusion that senior leadership is either not interested or is unable to provide the next phase of

strategic direction we need in order to keep elevating our performance to the next level."

You pause, catch your breath, and continue. "Kerry, I would be really interested in knowing what your thoughts and reactions are to my point of view. I don't know if it makes any sense to you. I know I don't get to see all of the interactions of the senior executives, but I would be interested to know if you think my perspective about the business has any merit."

Kerry is very quiet, and for a moment you think he may explode because you clearly described an opportunity for improvement. Normally, you are not that bold or open with him, probably because you have been living in the minimizing mode. You really tried to be objective. You really tried to control your tone, as Taylor has coached you to do. But you know you were taking a risk. You are feeling very vulnerable and hoping Kerry will not take your feedback the wrong way. After using the process for a while, you've learned that there are no guarantees about how others will react to your insights. Taylor has warned you many times that courageous coaching can sometimes be uncomfortable, and it certainly is in this case.

Kerry seems to gather his thoughts. Then he responds, "In the spirit of candor and openness, let me just say that you are partly right and partly wrong."

That is actually a better response than you had expected. For a moment, you thought Kerry was going to say you were all wrong.

"Help me understand what you mean," you respond.

Kerry says, "You are right in the sense that senior leadership has been missing in action when it comes to communicating key parts of the strategy. No all-employee town hall meetings have been held. No written communications about the strategy and vision have been distributed. No quarterly updates on business progress and feedback on business performance have been communicated. It is no surprise that some departments and functions are struggling to get their strategy aligned with senior leadership. Everyone deserves to know what senior leadership wants for the long term. The part that you are wrong about is the executive team's lack of work and conversation about the future.

"Thanks to some of the work they have seen occurring in your group, the executive team started meeting for four hours on a monthly basis to talk about how to position the business in the future, how to create a competitive advantage, and how to differentiate Galaxy from other up-and-coming pharma companies, among other topics. The meetings have been spirited and heated at times, but in the past few months, a consensus has developed. One topic has been whether or not to share the strategy with the rest of the company, fearing that this might be leaked to some of our competitors, suppliers, and customers. But Adrian, I think that your point is valid, and one way or another, this information is going to come out since we are a publicly traded company. There are no secrets. Furthermore, that strategy needs to be shared because some of the direction and long-term solutions have got to come from the bottom up. I don't think senior leadership has all the answers. It is the folks on the front lines talking to customers and suppliers who have the really important insight.

"So that is what I mean when I say that you are partly right and partly wrong. We have got to get a lot better at doing strategic work in every part of the business. I want to reassure you that the work you are doing with Marketing gives us courage and hope. We think we have an organization that has some natural strategic leaders, and we will need a lot of that going forward. You made it perfectly clear that we have to have more conversations, give people a template, and have open debate about where we need to take this business next."

Wow—that is a big relief. For a few minutes, you thought Kerry was going to fire you on the spot for being brazen and speaking your mind.

But to your surprise, Kerry then says, "Hey, I know that this is not easy. I know you have been sponsoring and championing a lot more candor and honesty about business issues, so Adrian, I have a higher opinion of you for speaking your mind. I can tell you have given this careful thought for a long time."

"I have been thinking about this for a really long time, and I have kept quiet about it. But I feel a lot better now that we've talked about it," you reply. Kerry thanks you for the productive meeting and then has to leave to catch a flight. It feels like you ended the dialogue in a good place. It felt good to use the skills you learned at another level, and you feel like you are getting better at it every time you have a candid conversation. But you know that you will have to continue doing it in order to keep your skill set sharp. You also know that others will continue looking to you as an example for help in this area.

It's evening; you reflect on the day's events and what has happened with Lee. While it hasn't necessarily been easy, from your point of view, good outcome has been built on a culture of communication and coaching that is open, transparent, and bold. Without the principles that were laid out that day with Taylor, everyone in the organization would be dancing around difficult topics and minimizing the realities of leading a young, growing company forward.

APPENDIX

The Courageous Conversations Workshop from CMOE

Courageous Conversations Defined

A courageous conversation is a discussion between two or more people about a difficult topic that uses a framework to help the conversation stay focused on the issue or problem and not on the personality or person. It is a way for caring, competent, hard-working people to have a meaningful discussion regarding difficult issues and bring about effective resolutions.

Why Courageous Conversations?

Managers and leaders face an assortment of daunting responsibilities they must accomplish to be effective in their roles. These responsibilities include providing rigorous performance feedback, making tough decisions under pressure, holding others accountable, and working as a

clear, vibrant conduit between senior management and the work force. When it comes to effectively performing these functions, one pivotal skill stands out above all the rest: the ability to foster direct, constructive dialogue—especially when engaging difficult, non-routine, and complex issues.

The Courageous Conversations Workshop is a thorough, skill-based approach to developing interpersonal competence. The workshop provides participants with competencies for reasoning and action for both individuals and teams. The skills and concepts presented are based on a tested methodology and backed by ongoing research. The Courageous Conversations Workshop is designed for participants to study current organizational problems as they learn the skills needed to overcome them.

Participants Will Learn How To:

- Identify organizational, team, and interpersonal situations that they find most problematic and recognize why their best efforts to deal with these situations are often ineffective.

- Conduct dynamic conversations with people in higher positions of authority so that critical bottom-up communication remains open and productive.

- Foster conditions that will enable people to act with high levels of candor, respect, and responsibility as they engage difficult, complex issues.

- Significantly reduce destructive finger-pointing and blaming when dealing with tough problems and issues, and keep people focused on the relevant issues.

- Apply new action models for advocacy and inquiry to real business issues.

- Develop precision questions to help elevate discussion and/or debate to the level of a skillful conversation.

The Coaching Skills™ Workshop from CMOE

Coaching Defined

Coaching is the ongoing process of building partnerships aimed at continuous improvement. It is a two-way communication process between members of the organization (e.g. leaders to team members, team members to leaders, and peer-to-peer) that is designed to develop and enhance hard and soft skills, motivation, attitude, judgment, and the ability to perform and contribute to an organization's strategic objectives.

Why Coaching Skills™?

The global economy has changed and presents today's leaders with more opportunities to coach for performance and results. Leaders who possess coaching skills directly impact current and future employee performance in

numerous ways. Leaders who acquire active coaching skills have the ability to enhance growth and performance, promote individual responsibility, and encourage accountability.

CMOE's Coaching TIPS²™ Workshop is designed to help participants develop the necessary skills to effectively coach others. The workshop is based on The Coaching TIPS²™ Model—a proven process that is backed by extensive and ongoing research. The Model is a flexible and dynamic communication road map that leaders use to interact more effectively in a coaching situation. The workshop also focuses on helping participants develop the following skills:

- Promoting a highly engaged work environment, a culture of trust, enhanced performance, and improved productivity.
- Sharing feedback on their performance and development.
- Coaching to achieve the full potential of team members and drive bottom-line results.
- Bringing resistance to change to the surface and working through obstacles (hidden or not) that impede change.
- Developing and enhancing execution skills to drive strategic priorities.
- Addressing performance problems through greater individual and team accountability.
- Developing future leadership talent by increasing innovation, commitment, and ownership.
- Building respect and trust among team members.

Learn more about CMOE's Coaching TIPS²™ and Coaching Skills™ Workshops and how they will benefit your organization by calling us at +1 801 569 3444, visiting us at www.CMOE.com and filling out our inquiry form, or by sending an e-mail to info@cmoe.com.

The Strategic Leadership Workshop from CMOE

Strategic Leadership Defined

Strategic Leadership is achieving a long-term competitive edge over your rivals by creating and delivering a compelling value proposition to the organization. It is being proficient at anticipating changes, opportunities, and challenges, and proactively shaping the future within an area of responsibility and influence. Strategic Leaders with an innovative and proactive mind are able to discover value-added solutions and find new ways to help the business grow.

Why Strategic Leadership?

More than ever before, organizations need strong, capable strategic leaders who can motivate, coach, and inspire people to do strategic work that will help ensure

the organization's success over the long term. Contributors at all levels in the organization look to their leaders for direction and clues as to how the future will unfold and how they can add distinctive value to the organization's success. In order to survive and thrive, organizations will have to navigate strategic shifts and develop new sources of competitive advantage for the firm. Therefore, leaders have to increase their focus and effectiveness, adapt to competitive pressures, and uncover hidden opportunities.

Leaders have a choice to make: they can look forward and take responsibility for identifying and planning for strategic opportunities and problems that will arise in the business environment, or they can muddle through and hope the future will be kind. However, hope is never a strategy. Leaders serve others and the organization best when they create strategic projects and plans, and then mobilize their resources towards proactively taking on the future.

For any organization to be strategically positioned, each function, department, and person will have to figure out how to align with, and support, the organization's overarching strategy. However, it is just as important that every leader create and execute their own unique, stand-alone strategy that is parallel with the business.

The Strategic Leadership Workshop provides leaders and managers with the skills and tools to help them successfully capitalize on the forces and events that shape their world, allowing them to become the architects of the future within their area of responsibility. This workshop will help leaders see the big picture and find new ways for their team to contribute maximum value over the long run by transforming their piece of the value chain and

operating from a more strategic point of reference while delivering on today's expectations.

Participants Will Learn How To:

- Balance the need to meet operational demands with creating innovative strategic initiatives that drive long-term performance and competitiveness.
- Incorporate business strategy skills and principles into their function.
- Complete a strategic analysis of their work area.
- Develop strategic priorities.
- Enroll others and build commitment to the construction and implementation of strategies—be it at the individual, team, departmental, or business unit level.
- Manage distractions and allocate time for strategic thinking and action.
- Identify and leverage key competitive advantages and strategic innovations.
- Create Strategic Measures of Effectiveness™ in order to measure and track progress towards specific strategic initiatives.

To learn more about CMOE's Strategic Leadership Workshop and how it will benefit your organization, call us at +1 801 569 3444, visit us at www.CMOE.com and fill out an inquiry form, or send an e-mail to info@cmoe.com.

The Applied Strategic Thinking® Workshop from CMOE

Strategic Thinking Defined

Strategic thinking is gathering information and looking towards the future in order to anticipate events before they happen and to recognize emerging trends, opportunities, and risks. Strategic thinkers proactively invest in actions and plans that will pay off in the future. Strategic thinking requires some risk-taking, innovation, experience, and intuition.

Why Applied Strategic Thinking®?

We live and work in a fast-paced, turbulent, and changing environment with many opportunities, uncertainties, and hazards. Managers and individual contributors alike frequently become preoccupied with day-to-day tactics and fail to prepare for the long-term or position them-

selves for success in the future. It is vital that all members of the organization feel responsible for achieving organizational results, have a broad perspective, and are aware of the trends and developments shaping their work. With a little discipline and thought, managers and individual contributors can develop the ability to gain, expand, and exercise greater influence over their work and make a strategic contribution to their organization. The challenge today is to find a way to see the future in a sea of change.

Strategic thinking is sometimes viewed as a complex and intimidating topic. However, thinking strategically is simply having the skills and foresight to solve tomorrow's problems today. We believe that this kind of strategic thinking can benefit leaders and teams in all types of organizations, as well as individuals who want to truly ignite positive change in their areas of responsibility.

The Applied Strategic Thinking® Workshop will teach participants how to think, plan, and act more strategically at the individual level and on the front lines of work. Using real-life experiences, illustrated examples, straightforward activities, and time-tested tools, the Applied Strategic Thinking® Workshop provides the necessary skills to help leaders and individual contributors become strategically minded and forward-thinking.

Participants Will Learn How To:

- Define "Applied Strategic Thinking" and the principles that go with it.
- Develop the skills necessary to think and act at a strategic level.
- Align and link individual strategies with the overall organizational strategy.

- Identify and exploit opportunities.
- Analyze strengths and weaknesses.
- Successfully capitalize on forces and events that shape their life and work.
- Gather and use intelligence data.
- Analyze the changes happening today that will influence tomorrow's results.
- Accelerate and sustain strategic initiatives.

Every organization needs more strategic thinkers. Learn more about the Applied Strategic Thinking® Workshop by calling us at +1 801 569 3444, visiting us at www.CMOE.com (fill out an inquiry form to send us your contact information), or by sending an e-mail to info@cmoe.com.

The Strategic Teamwork™ Workshop from CMOE

Teamwork Defined

A unified group of individuals who work together, share information, and combine their energy and expertise to achieve extraordinary strategic results. A group in which team members understand their strategic responsibilities and are prepared to give the group their best performance in order to achieve long-term success for the team and organization.

Why Strategic Teamwork?

There are many types of work groups and teams that exist in organizations. Few, however, function strategically. Because strategic teamwork can be challenging to achieve, CMOE's Strategic Teamwork Workshop assists teams with transforming into a strategic team and confronting core issues such as setting strategic direction, aligning

team member efforts, tapping into creativity, maximizing resources, ensuring accountability, dealing with strategic change in a positive way, and increasing productivity.

Strategic Teamwork is a powerful, experienced-based workshop that shows participants how to build and sustain a high-performance strategy team, as well as how to develop teamwork and strategy skills at the individual level. The experiential nature of the training, combined with adult learning methods, ensures an exciting and memorable event. Participants walk away with an integrated set of skills, knowledge, and plans to renew team spirit, enhance performance through strategic thinking, and improve the long-term contribution of the team so it adds distinctive value to the organization now and in the future. When these skills are applied, teams are stronger, more productive, and more aligned in purpose than ever before.

The Strategic Teamwork Workshop is tailored for intact teams, cross-functional teams, or a mixed group of individuals. The workshop is customized to each organization's specific team issues and needs.

Participants Will Learn How To:

- Have an exciting learning experience that will raise their level of interest in and commitment to strategic teamwork.

- Discover new methods to enhance the team's ability to make a strategic contribution and produce creative solutions to team challenges.

- Explore ways to build team motivation and revitalize commitment to the team's strategy.

- Take-away tools and resources that will instill team cohesiveness and strategic alignment.
- Gain personal insight about how their individual actions and behaviors either add to or detract from strategic teamwork.
- Understand the:
  - Role and value of team leadership in achieving long-term results.
  - Necessity of effective personal and interpersonal communication.
  - Ways to utilize the resources and talents within the team.
  - Importance of strategy and vision.
  - Methods of problem-solving and of handling conflict and differences.

Titles by CMOE Press

- *Strategy is Everyone's Job: A Guide to Strategic Leadership*
- *Courageous Coaching Conversations: How to be Bold and Clear When it Really Matters*
- *The Coach: Creating Partnerships for a Competitive Edge*
- *Win-Win Partnerships: Be on the Leading Edge with Synergistic Coaching*
- *The Team Approach: With Teamwork Anything is Possible*
- *Leading Groups to Solutions: A Practical Guide for Facilitators and Team Members*
- *Ahead of the Curve: A Guide to Applied Strategic Thinking*
- *Teamwork: We Have Met the Enemy and They are Us*

To order, call +1 801 569 3444 or visit us online at www.CMOE.com.

Connect and Continue the Journey

Visit and Comment on CMOE's Blog
http://www.cmoe.com/blog

Download CMOE's Express Coaching App
http://goo.gl/iI77k

Connect with CMOE on LinkedIn
http://www.linkedin.com/company/cmoe

Connect with CMOE on Google+
http://goo.gl/BZNmX

Connect with CMOE on Facebook
http://www.facebook.com/CMOE.inc

Connect with CMOE on Twitter
http://mobile.twitter.com/cmoe

Connect with CMOE on Pinterest
http://pinterest.com/cmoeinc/

Connect with CMOE on Quora
http://www.quora.com/Steve-Stowell

www.CMOE.com